What executives are saying about Gary Patterson:

" Gary Patterson provides the fiscal checkup that every business needs to stay healthy. His insightful points convey meaningful advice that can boost productivity and keep expenses in line."

    Dr. Nido Qubein, President, High Point University
    Chairman, Great Harvest Bread Co.

" No matter what size company you lead, this practical and resourceful book will help you turn your business strategies into high performance results."

    Pamela S. Harper, President Business Advancement Inc.
    Author, Preventing Strategic Gridlock® (Cameo Publications)

" Gary's no-nonsense approach concentrates on insights that will improve all aspects of a company's strategic thinking, budget planning, and risk management. Here, he provides decision makers with recession-proof tools, strategies, and resources that will help them transform challenges into opportunities."

    James C. Cantalini, President of Torsted Advisors
    former CEO of Gist Communications, Inc.

" As a CEO of a high-growth company, I have found Gary's counsel, insights, and best practices essential. I continue to follow his advice and methods. Gary's the real deal. **Stick Out Your Balance Sheet** is required reading for every CEO running a high-growth company."

    Dean Macri, CEO
    Cielo Mobile Inc.

" *Engaging and accessible, Gary's best practices give you the tools and resources you need to navigate through these uncertain times."*

>David J. Roache, Managing Director,
>connectC

" *A book that makes good common sense yet is not commonly applied. A great handyman's guide full of practical information that you'll want to keep nearby for constant reminders of following the right steps BEFORE it's too late."*

>Richard Dauphinais, President
>Strategic Compensation Partners

" *Gary is a no bias, no bull financial go-to guy. A quick study, he has the ability to identify systemic financial bugaboos and offer spot-on solutions that put companies back on track to growth and profitability."*

>Leigh A. McGee, Co-Founder
>OSIYO Consulting LLC

Stick Out Your Balance Sheet and Cough

Best Practices for Long-Term Business Health

by
Gary W. Patterson
The FiscalDoctor®

STICK OUT YOUR BALANCE SHEET AND COUGH:
Best practices for long-term business health

Copyright © 2009 by Gary W. Patterson. All rights reserved. No part of this book may be used or reproduced in any manner whatsoever without written permission except in the case of brief quotations in articles and reviews. FiscalDoctor® is a registered trademark of Gary W. Patterson.

Portions of Chapter 8, "Stress Test: Show Me the Data (on Time!)" were first published in *Directors Monthly*, February 2008, "Get the Board Data You Need on Time" and is reprinted with permission of the publisher, National Association of Corporate Directors, 1133 21st Street, NW, Washington, DC 20036 (www.nacdonline.org).

Portions of Chapter 10, "The Price of Going Green: The Good and Not So Good," were first published in *Financial Executive*, November 2007, "How Will You Cope in a Clean Energy World?" and is reprinted with permission of Financial Executives International; 200 Campus Drive, Florham Park, NJ 07932-0674; 973.765.1000; (www.financialexecutives.org).

Portions of Chapter 11, "How Fiscally Fit Does Your Board of Directors Think You Are?" were first published in *Directors & Boards,* Fall 2007, " What Is Your Board's Embarrassment IQ?" and is reprinted with permission of Directors & Boards, 1845 Walnut Street, Suite 900, Philadelphia, PA 19103 (www.directorsandboards.com).

These prior articles have been updated and expanded, and as such are the responsibility of the author.

Photograph is reprinted with the permission of Nancy Carbonaro.

ISBN-13: 978-0-9822415-0-9

FIRST EDITION • Printed in the U.S.A.
13 12 11 10 09   5 4 3 2 1

Published by FiscalClinic Communications,
a division of FiscalDoctor, Inc.

For reprint permission or additional copies of this book visit:
www.fiscaldoctor.com

Many Thanks...

I would like to offer my sincere appreciation and thanks to the following people. Without them this book would not be what it is. Chris Adams, Chad Barr, Chere Bork, Vickie Bouffard, Roni Briggs, Sara Lou Brown, Rosemary Brutico, Matt Bud, David Butler, James Cantalini, Nancy Carbonaro, Nancy Carey, Greg Carney, Stuart Darsch, Richard Dauphinais, David Fater, Steven Feldman, Elaine Floyd, Joseph Gallagher, Larry Grumer, Jack Hanna, Pamela Harper, Douglas Hubbard, Tom Kennedy, James Kristie, Anthony Kubica, Lawrence Kutner, Alexandra Lajoux, Steven Ledgerwood, Gerard Lorden, Dean Macri, Brent Mathews, Bruce McCuaig, John Martinson, Roberta Matuson, Leigh Ann McGee, Eugene Mehr, Douglas Miller, Gary Milleson, Mary Anne North, Robert Norton, Ralph Norwood, Christen, Gary Jr. and Katherine Patterson, Ed Pendergast, Adele Pollis, Nido Qubein, Mel Prenovitz, David Roache, Lee Roberts, Lawrence Siff, Martha Slaight, Phil Symchych, Rich Tarnopolski, Libby Wagner, Alan Weiss, and David and Denise Williams for their talents and insights.

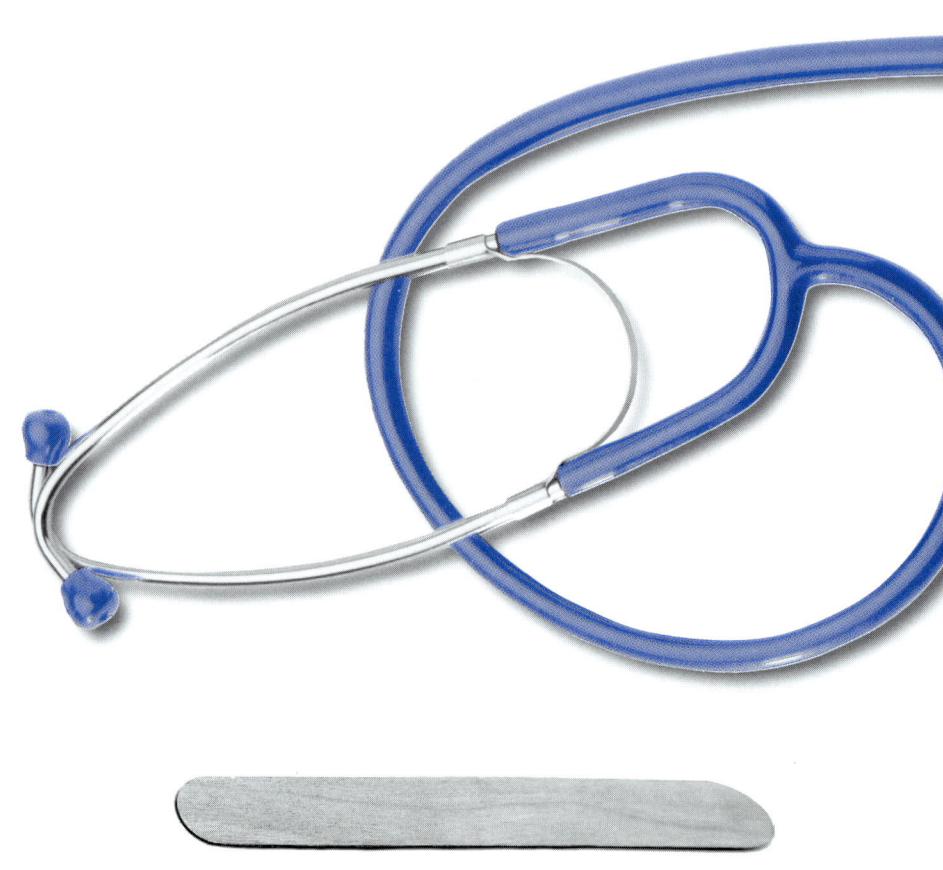

*There is a great deal of difference
between the eager man who wants to read a book
and the tired man who wants a book to read.*

–G. K. Chesterton

Table of Contents

Introduction 9

1. Take the FiscalDoctor's Test 19
2. Your Fiscal Vision Is the Heart of Your Growth Strategy 27
3. What Is Your Appetite for Risk? 41
4. The Internal Exam: Five Areas Where Risk Can Lurk 51
5. Healthy Reserves: Why Cash Is King 61
6. How Fit Is Your Business Model? 69
7. Breathe New Life Into Your Pricing Model 79
8. Stress Test: Show Me the Data (on Time!) 91
9. ER: When Bad Things Happen to Good Companies 101
10. The Price of Going Green: The Good and Not So Good 113
11. How Fiscally Fit Does Your Board of Directors Think You Are? 121

Resources: The Doctor's Bag 129

*A smooth sea never made a skillful mariner;
neither do uninterrupted prosperity and success
qualify for usefulness and happiness.
The storms of adversity, like those of the ocean,
rouse the faculties and excite the invention...
and prudence of the voyager.*

–Unknown

Introduction

Unlike other books that are written for multibillion-dollar companies, *Stick Out Your Balance Sheet and Cough* is targeted to CEOs and business leaders of young to middle-market companies who are managing growth while struggling with the reality of these challenging economic times. The practices I offer in these pages will not only help you weather the economic turmoil, but equally important, will better prepare you to seize the opportunities that lie before you despite the times.

While business pundits are quick to compare the current global financial collapse of venerable institutions to the Great Depression, I stand behind the sentiment of Franklin Delano Roosevelt when his inaugural address roused a nation steeped in despair with these words, "The only thing we have to fear is fear itself." On that note, I believe that many great companies are born and rise to the top in economic times like these. The financial rewards will go to those leaders who are willing to stare down fear and forge ahead with their vision of prosperity and unbounded opportunity.

At the end of the day, my goal as the FiscalDoctor is to help CEOs, entrepreneurs, executive teams, and shareholders sleep better at night knowing their companies are on the path to greater profitability and long-term financial fitness and well-being. The companies that "get it" know they need the proper fiscal (financial, operations and systems) mindset, which is covered in the FiscalDoctor's test in Chapter 1. Unfortunately, most businesses use accounting systems and reports that are *historical* in nature instead of offering current and relevant information needed for management to run the business.

Such a backward-looking approach can result in devastating inventory problems, inadequate purchase order controls, crippling vendor contracts, and giveaway sales reductions. In contrast, this book offers a "Doctor's Bag" of the essential instruments, tools, and frameworks a decision maker needs to evaluate the financial fitness of his or her organization *going forward*, along with a treatment plan that will develop a mindset of financial preparedness.

The $30-Million Time Bomb: A Case Study

To begin, let's look at how the contents of the Doctor's Bag helped one company avoid a near-fatal situation. Without revealing the company's name, let's just say it was a $40-million, high-flying Inc. 500 company that had revolutionized the luggage industry. Its claim to fame was putting wheels on suitcases. I was brought in as CFO to bring the company public – what most CFOs would consider a dream job. It didn't take long for the dream to turn into a nightmare.

The Patient Profile: I joined the company right after it had completed its financial audit. Merrill Lynch's then commercial lending arm had given the company an increased line of credit for several million dollars for a major capital expansion to prepare it for the IPO planned for the following year. Within the first two weeks, Merrill Lynch asked me to update the financial projections from what people often call dream (a.k.a. phantom) numbers to realistic five-year projections.

By week three, I discovered a financial oversight that would have undone the company. This $40-million company had recently placed inventory orders for $30-million worth of suitcases scheduled to arrive over the next six months. As unbelievable as it sounds, situations of this magnitude relative to corporate size periodically occur in companies too focused on growth to be bothered by monitoring risk. Also, scenarios like this go a long way toward explaining why executives and board members are beginning to emphasize risk management equally with corporate governance. They have no desire to be featured in a future *Wall Street Journal* article on some ignored formerly invisible risk that explodes at the worst possible time.

Supposedly, no one in management knew about this imbalance or how it happened. Worse than that, the company didn't have the money to pay for it, nor did it have the storage space for the inventory. And, it was purchasing the wrong inventory to boot. So, why not just stop the order and refuse to pay? The suitcases were already being manufactured overseas, and I was told the purchase order could not be canceled without destroying vendor relations and, most likely, launching unwanted lawsuits.

The Symptoms: Management was in denial. Initially, they couldn't even believe it was true that such a situation could have happened in their company, on their watch. The general reaction was: "Gary, I am shocked. We think you're a sharp guy, but go back and check the numbers again." So I burrowed even deeper into the numbers secretly hoping my startling first numbers were wrong. But after two more intensive secretive weeks, I came back with the same $30-million problem, summarized in a detailed spreadsheet. What became obvious was that the company lacked a reliable financial system that captured the company's inventory transactions. Like too many other accounting systems and the reports they deliver, this company was relying on historical data instead of offering current and relevant information needed for management to run the business for today, let alone for tomorrow.

This is a classic case of a company mistaking bean counting for actual management. The inventory orders would have eventually shown up—as a footnote in the following year's audit—but, they were not included in the company's financial projections.

By the time the next audit rolled around, the company itself would have been history. Visions of career embarrassment, liquidity problems, broken dreams, missed bonuses, employee layoffs, the forced sale of the company, corporate bankruptcy, and even the potential loss of the founder's home, which secured the corporate guarantee, replayed along with other nightmares going through our heads as we grappled with the gravity of the situation. And, as with most problems lurking deep within a company, the inventory problem was just the tip of the iceberg masking other "accountability, reporting, and management" issues that lay under the surface.

Using what evolved into the FiscalDoctor method, I performed the following:

The Checkup: Upon examination, it became clear the company didn't have a sound business plan that included real financial projections. The company was operating with "wishful" numbers and a false feeling of general well-being, rather than a strategic business plan. Additionally, there was limited or no contingency planning format, versions of which are now called Enterprise Risk Management (ERM).

The Diagnosis: The $30-million time bomb needed to be addressed immediately, not during the following year's audit and not two or three years in the future. This meant the company had to obtain financing and improve cash flow over the next few months to pay for the inventory purchases. Otherwise the company would be in dire financial straits, which would have threatened its IPO position, if not the survival of the company.

The Treatment Plan: Stanch the bleeding. In other words, you must control the damage and prevent the problem from getting bigger. When the owner asked what it would take to contain the problem, I responded that we needed to hire another person to help me. My options were to hire either an accountant who didn't know much about inventory or an inventory person who didn't know accounting. Based on the daunting inventory issues to be addressed, I chose the latter. Together the new hire and I worked as a team with the controller. We found a number of creative strategies to work with different departments, particularly purchasing, inventory, sales and operations departments.

The Prescription:

○ **First, we put purchase order controls in place** to ensure that we would only be buying inventory that we needed. This included analyzing our stock needs vis-à-vis our sales history and sales projections to determine which models of suitcases were selling at the level of our projections. Working on a shoestring budget to compensate for an inadequate software system (debits did not have to equal credits, which we also solved), we created a series of basic Excel models to highlight those inventory areas where the purchasing and sales departments could stop the inventory profit leaks. Specifically, this calculated the number of day's sales of each product on hand in warehouse inventory. Generally our maximum allowable inventory level on any item was set at seven months stock on hand. In other words, items could not be reordered until its average days sales fell below seven months.

○ **Second, we looked at our $30-million commitment** to see how we could renegotiate the purchase order contracts with our various suppliers. Although we were told that we were locked into our commitment, we worked with purchasing, and we were able to convert orders for some poor-selling models to orders for top-selling models, where we actually needed additional orders. The key lesson here is that everything is negotiable. We see that again in the down economy.

○ **Third, the team worked with the sales force** to determine the best way to move our inventory by generating overstock sales or other discounted methods.

In less than a year, the inventory glut was cut by $15 million. This put us in a much better position to find a new lender who offered us a substantially increased loan line. This allowed us to pay for the incoming inventory at the same time that the company was selling its way back to some level of normality.

Overall Wellness Plan. The business plan we created during this process gave us the road map we needed to gradually dig out of the problem. The bleeding was stopped, profit leaks were plugged, inventory controls were in place and management had the information they needed to plan forward, instead of just reflect backward. And, how does the story end? The company is still in business today.

The FiscalDoctor Is In

While your company may not face the same kind of looming financial disaster as the luggage company, chances are you could benefit from a checkup by the FiscalDoctor. After all, the management team at the luggage company didn't even know they needed intensive care attention.

This book is written to keep your company out of a similar fiscal emergency. Like an emergency room triage, the FiscalClinic© offers four key areas of service designed to determine your fiscal health. FiscalClinic can be used as a comprehensive system or used individually as needed. After you complete the triage, you'll know whether you're healthy and rarin' to go, whether you need an aspirin and a bandage or two, or whether you need to call in a specialist for serious emergency care. The areas of service are:

Checkup: This high-level overview identifies immediate issues (a.k.a. ailments or symptoms) that need to be resolved to help you better understand your company's current financial situation. Take your company's pulse now and ask yourself: *Is it fundamentally weak or strong?* Then listen more closely to the beat.

Diagnosis: Identify the risks and opportunities you face in your efforts to grow and sustain your company through a more focused analysis and review of your company's financial and operating systems, or what can be termed your company's lifeblood. How well does the blood flow to the company's vital organs (suppliers, customers, employees, shareholders)? Where are the blockages, and how do we eliminate them? Where are the openings, and how do we enhance them? In essence, the FiscalClinic diagnosis gives you the framework for better managing the challenges and risks inherent in growing your business.

Treatment: Use your checkup and diagnosis as a guide to develop a treatment plan for good health (a.k.a. risk contingency strategy) based on your company's internal strengths and weaknesses vis-à-vis the external environment. Using your vision for the future as a starting point, your treatment plan will bolster strengths, minimize weaknesses and put you in a position to seize market opportunities as they arise.

Wellness: Develop a daily regimen of good health based on a contingency plan that allows you to adapt to changes in the marketplace while helping you stay the course and remain true to your goals and visions. As any good doctor knows, a prescription comes with a general wellness plan and follow-up services. As such, I offer advisory services to help maintain your company's financial health and support your business goals for growth and profitability. My wellness plan could include acting as consultant or in limited cases as an interim CFO.

For Best Results, Use the Best Practices as Directed

Over 200 companies have benefited from the FiscalDoctor's Best Practices as they traversed the often challenging path to growth and profitability. In this book, I present these Best Practices to you with the sincere hope that you will use them to grow your company into an efficient, fiscally fit organization that embodies your goals and visions.

May your company be well and may you sleep tight.

Sincerely,
Gary W. Patterson
April 2009

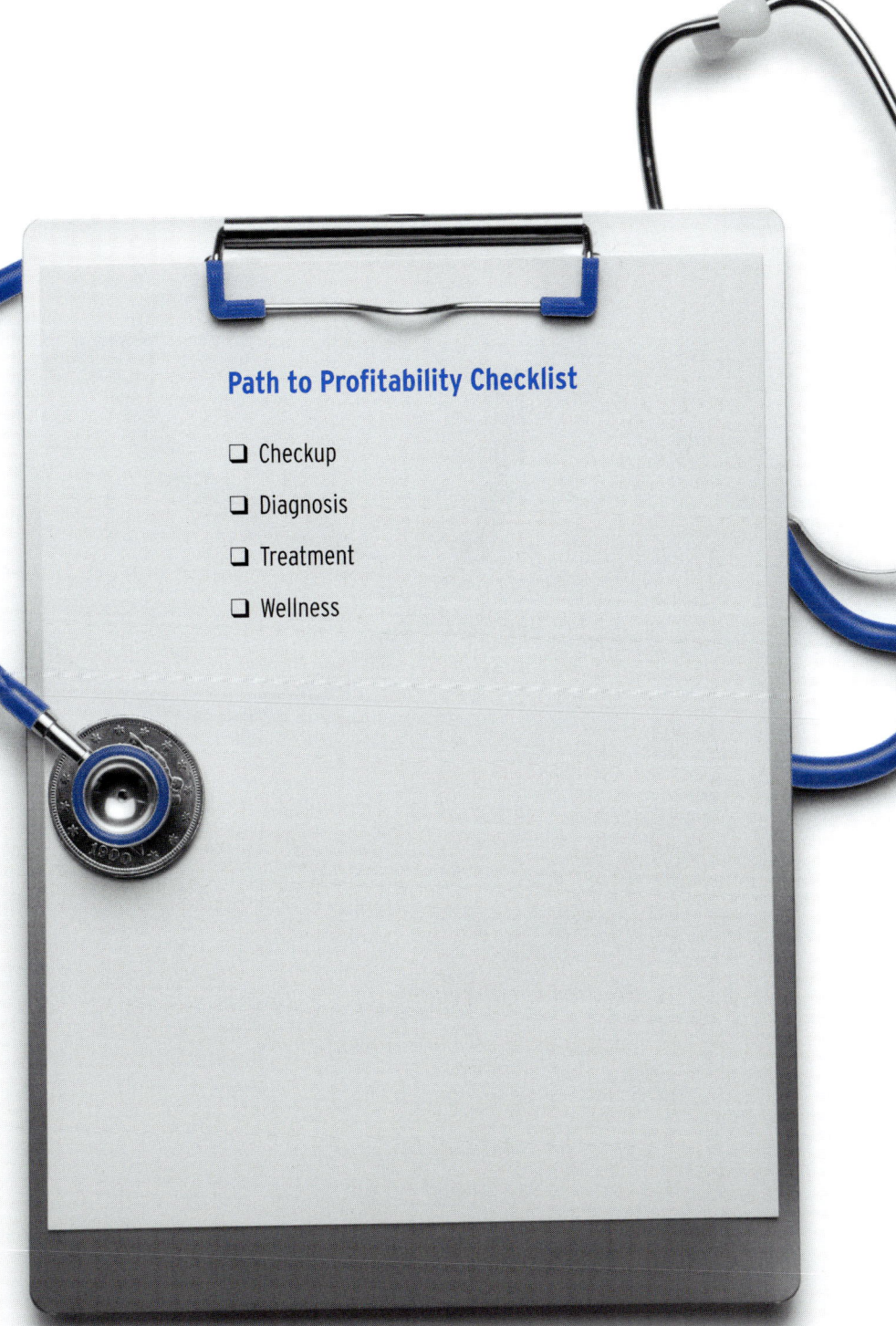

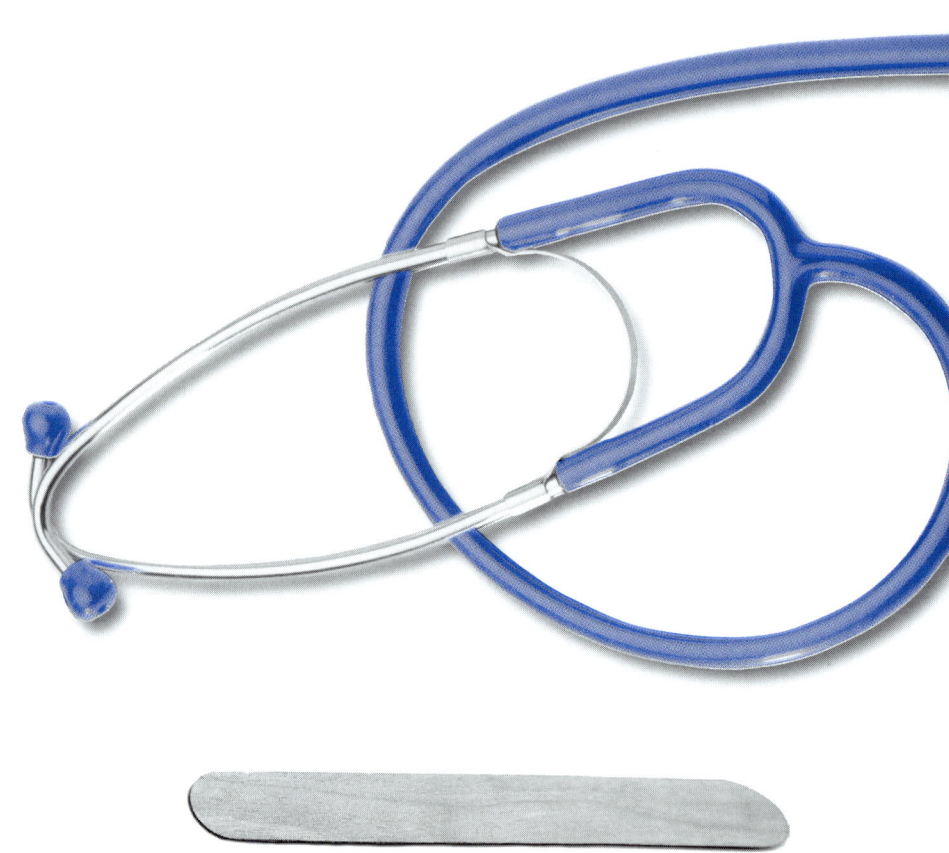

If a man will begin with certainties,
he shall end in doubts;
but if he will be content to begin with doubts,
he shall end in certainty.

–Francis Bacon

Take the FiscalDoctor's Test

First, the nurse tells you to step on the scales. Then he or she will take your blood pressure and ask you to pee in a cup. They don't do these things for their own amusement when you show up for a checkup. They do them because they need to establish a baseline or compare your health today to your health at your last visit. So, before you dive in, skip ahead, or even put this book aside for a later time, I strongly urge you to take the time to complete the FiscalDoctor test.

The results of the test will be helpful on two levels. One, and most important, it will reveal the fiscal fitness of your company. Two, it will serve as a guide to help you navigate the chapters of the book. For example, based on your answers, you may want to go directly to the chapters that pertain to the most serious issues and challenges you face.

I've also left space below the questions for you to write your answers to the questions "why" and "why not," so you can refer to them time and time again as you're reading the book. So, step on the scales, dear reader and tell me truthfully, "How fiscally fit is your company?"

1. Are operations running so smoothly at your company that you consistently sleep well at night?

    ○ Yes   ○ No

Why?

Why Not?

2. Are you REALLY sure your balance sheet is an accurate recording of your business TODAY?

⭘ Yes   ⭘ No

Why?

Why Not?

3. Are you satisfied with your capability to project available cash over the next six months?

⭘ Yes   ⭘ No

Why?

Why Not?

4. Are the key facts and measurements you need to run your business and accomplish strategic objectives readily available?

⭘ Yes   ⭘ No

Why?

Why Not?

5. Do you operate from at least a three-year strategic plan?

⭘ Yes   ⭘ No

Why?

Why Not?

Take the FiscalDoctor's Test

6. Are you confident that your company will be able to meet your targeted growth in revenues and profits over the next three years?

    ○ Yes   ○ No

Why?

Why Not?

7. Do your competitors see you as their primary competition?

    ○ Yes   ○ No

Why?

Why Not?

8. Does your company stack up well against other companies in your industry in terms of fundamental financial measurements, such as: gross profit %; net profit %; cash flow; average days receivables outstanding; average days inventory on hand; bad debt loss %; and return on equity?

    ○ Yes   ○ No

Why?

Why Not?

9. Are you in a position to finance your growth plans?

    ○ Yes   ○ No

Why?

Why Not?

10. Do you really know your top ten customers both in terms of revenue and total profitability?

        ○ Yes   ○ No

Why?

Why Not?

11. Does everyone in your management team understand and support your corporate vision the same way you do?

        ○ Yes   ○ No

Why?

Why Not?

12. Are you in a position to seize market opportunities?

        ○ Yes   ○ No

Why?

Why Not?

13. Are you pleased with how your customers rate your company's performance?

        ○ Yes   ○ No

Why?

Why Not?

14. Are you seen as a successful leader who can make decisive and effective decisions?

        ○ Yes   ○ No

Why?

Why Not?

15. Does your management team think creatively? Are they "out-of-the box" thinkers?

   ○ Yes   ○ No

   Why?

   Why Not?

16. God forbid, but if you got hit by a bus tomorrow, do you have a trusted lieutenant who can keep your company on track?

   ○ Yes   ○ No

   Why?

   Why Not?

17. Do your vendors see you as a preferred customer, showing how well they value your relationship and business?

   ○ Yes   ○ No

   Why?

   Why Not?

18. Does your management team feel they receive information about your company and operations in an understandable and timely format to run their departments?

   ○ Yes   ○ No

   Why?

   Why Not?

19. Is your company prepared for the green economy?

   ○ Yes   ○ No

   Why?

   Why Not?

20. Are you aware of at least one improvement or a change in your company that would significantly enhance the performance of your company?

   ○ Yes   ○ No

   Why?

   Why Not?

See the scoring procedures to the right and tally your score. Unless you got a perfect score, one thing's for sure: You now know there are gaps in your ability to manage your company. Now that you know where you stand, you need to go back and reflect on your "no" answers to get a better understanding of the areas where you need to improve. These represent the gaps we seek to identify, diagnose, and treat.

 Coming Up

Your next step is to budget time to read the following chapters in this book. You're going to be very excited about how these Best Practices are going to help you reposition your company on the path to greater profitability,

Scoring Procedure:

Give yourself 5 points for each "yes." A no answer gets a 0 point. The scorecard shows where you stand.

Score	Comments
90-100	Excellent. Would you like to contribute a quote for the next edition of my book?
80–89	Above average
70–79	Average
60–69	Poor, need to improve
0–59	Situation CRITICAL, read book cover to cover

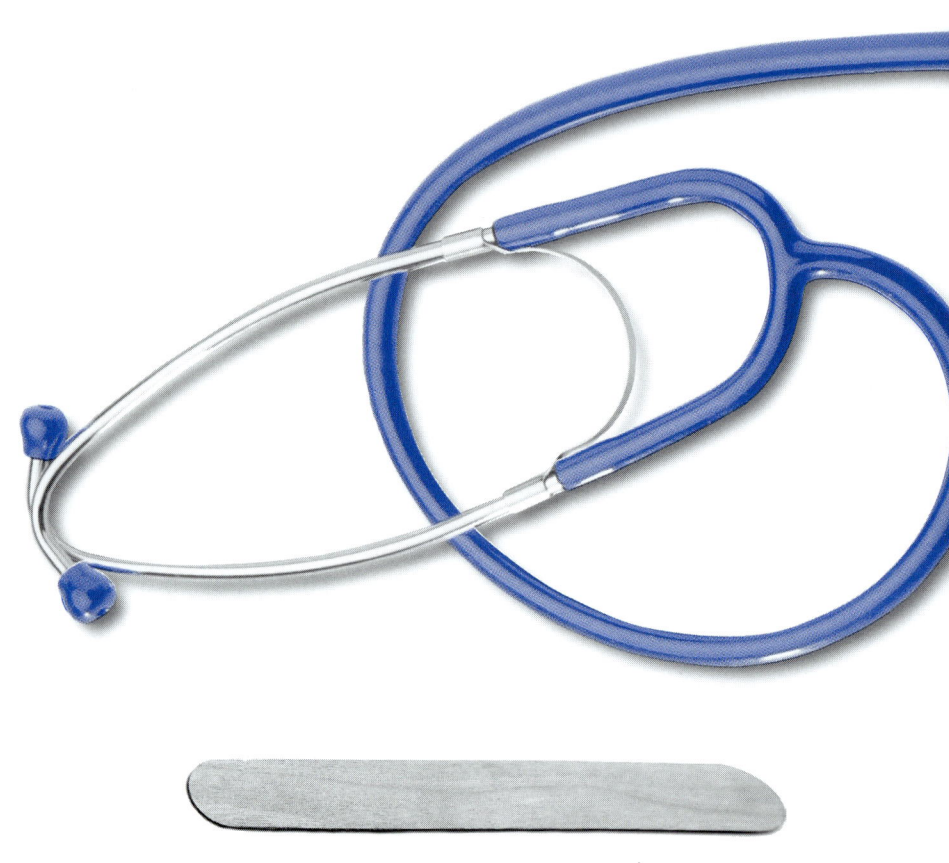

*A pessimist sees the difficulty in every opportunity;
an optimist sees the opportunity in every difficulty.*

—Winston Churchill

Your Fiscal Vision Is the Heart of Your Growth Strategy

As a high-growth consultant, when I'm brought into an organization it usually means one thing: The top decision maker, whether it be the founder, CEO, executive team, or investor, knows that he or she needs to do "something *new* or *different*" to keep the company growing in order to gain or sustain competitive advantage.

However, as you would expect, growing a business means different things to different executives depending on the underlying challenges, issues, and motivational drivers. Typically, when an executive articulates the need to grow, it suggests he or she is confronting or addressing one or more of the following situations:

- On the positive side, it reflects the CEO's confidence to periodically check to ensure that momentum will continue toward achieving the company's defined goals. After all, even companies that are doing well can benefit from an annual physical to ensure that their fiscal vision is still fiscally fit.

- On the negative side, it suggests that the CEO has a general gut feeling that something is not exactly right or a more serious concern that something is wrong or going wrong.

- Or, there are other serious concerns already identified, such as:
    - an inability to meet financial targets and/or corporate goals;
    - a sense that marketplace opportunities are being missed;

- an inability to obtain accurate and timely financial data to run the business proactively;

- a recurring crisis or series of "fire-fighting" incidents;

- or, concerns expressed by his or her law firm or accountant that "something is rotten in the state of Denmark."

Fiscal Vision: The Framework

A growth strategy without a fiscal vision is like a plane without wings. Unless you have a fiscal vision, growing your company is an endeavor that just won't get off the ground now no matter how hard you try. A fiscal vision comprises the decision maker's motivating factors, recognition of resources obtainable for finance, human resources, operations, and systems, and a critical review of your current business model. Embedded in a company's fiscal vision are an organization's values, which have to do with ingrained attitudes. (This is different from a decision maker's motivating factors, which are easier to change.)

Here's a quick example: Let's say we're competitors and we both have a motivating factor to be the leader in our industry. The biggest difference in our two companies is that I value paying people market rates and you value paying people above market. This value, relating to how we "value" and compensate our employees, along with a myriad of other types of value issues, subtly impacts every aspect of our fiscal visions and will affect our ability to compete in the marketplace.

Creating a fiscal vision for your company is a Best Practice process consisting of five building blocks that form a framework for customizing a growth strategy tailored to the unique issues and challenges you face. Similar to a growth strategy, a fiscal vision for a lifestyle company (a company where the primary business purpose is to provide the owners or management with comfortable life styles versus maximizing growth, profitability) looks very different from a company that is positioning itself for an IPO, or a large, traditional company that is losing its competitive edge and needs to re-engineer its business model. The bottom line is that in order for you to execute your growth strategy, you must first develop your fiscal vision.

Fiscal Vision: Defined

A fiscal vision blends accounting, finance, operations, and systems attributes used to improve, even accelerate a company's particular position. It is tailored to each decision maker's area of responsibility based upon that leader's goals, risk tolerance, access to resources, and time frame. A fiscal vision allows a decision maker to:

1. Clearly articulate the goals of the company and the under lying motivating factors driving the company's goals. This step is crucial in gaining the support and buy-in of the executive team and board of directors. If you can not clearly articulate the company's fiscal vision, you're going to have a difficult time getting your team and other stakeholders (e.g., employees, investors, vendors, and suppliers) to rally behind you and support your growth;

2. Identify and understand the resources required to obtain that goal or dream;

3. Better understand and be able to explain the level of risk required to reach that goal;

4. Better ensure the team creates or maintains a valid viable business model; and

5. Obtain operating data in a time frame and manner that supports management in these processes.

After going through the process of developing a fiscal vision, many executives will see budgets, profit margins, and cash flow in a new light. Because this process often results in changes or clarification of the existing business framework, you can be as creative or as flexible as you want in determining which step to use to start the process. The initial brainstorming framework normally expands into whatever area the decision maker identifies as needing the most improvement.

Step 1: Brainstorming Session

You've probably heard the axiom, "If you don't know where you're going, any road will get you there." Well, in business, it is more realistic to say "If you don't know where you're going, you're going nowhere." Planning, in other words, is essential to business success. However, while a fiscal vision is essential, it is just as essential to recognize that visions and strategies are not set in stone.

To develop a realistic fiscal vision, the executive team needs to come together to discuss the financial issues facing the company. As a key decision maker, however, you should review the questions below before bringing your executive team together. And, as the FiscalDoctor, I recommend you answer the questions briefly—a gut check, if you will, then read through the expanded version of the questions and, finally, go back and check your answers. Once you have briefly (and with brutal honesty!) answered these five fundamental questions, you will be in a much better position to lead your executive team toward the fiscal vision that will get you on the road to growth. In later chapters, you will expand on these initial answers and explore optimal ways to bring your team into the discussions to develop and then execute these ideas.

Your Fiscal Vision
is the Heart
of Your Growth Strategy

1. Why do you want to grow the company?

2. Why is this business a great opportunity?

3. What is your time frame for growing the company?

4. How are you going to fund the next two quarters?

5. Where is your company financially?

1. Why do you want to grow the company?
Often, decision makers have not focused on the emotional reasons they are building the company. For example, is it for industry recognition, fame, maximizing wealth in a certain time frame, or providing a philanthropic service or product to benefit some group or cause? This question sets the stage and is important for two other reasons: One, it spotlights the underlying motivation for why a founder and/or CEO has the need to grow the company; and two, it's a way for the founder and/or top decision maker to clarify misunderstandings with his or her management team on why a certain growth strategy is being executed. This question also helps to clarify attendant questions that will undoubtedly arise, such as what is meant by "growth?" Does growth have something to do with the company's competitive position, either negatively or positively?

2. Why is this business a great opportunity?
It is much cheaper to question the size of returns available from a business or product at an early or middle stage of a company's life than it is to wait until significant amounts of money, time, and scarce corporate resources have been committed to the business opportunity. In young growth companies people use the phrase, "Will the dogs eat the dog food?" to ascertain if the business opportunity is great, a dud, or just a so-so idea that

probably is not worth pursuing if better capital expenditure (CAPEX) opportunities exist.

For example, has the executive identified a unique opportunity just over the horizon? The idea for the personal computer was a great opportunity, a mediocre one, or a dud depending on when the concept was introduced. Some of you may have read about the Osborne portable computer that started as a great opportunity, was overtaken in the market and became a flop, all in a fairly short period of time. The ability to honestly and accurately evaluate your business opportunity at this particular time is absolutely essential to your success.

If it's an opportunity and/or a new venture scenario, the decision maker must understand the risks involved in undertaking the new venture and/or the risks involved in missing the opportunity, as well as the barrier to entry costs, expansion and new market costs, and how long it will take the company to make a profit from the new venture. If it's a competitive positioning scenario, the executive must be able to articulate the company's short- and long-term business goals.

3. *What is your time frame for growing the company?*

When working with clients, I "watch for cues" revealing unspoken agendas here. The time frame can be your time frame for your own reasons; a window in the market that is the driving force; or a combination of both factors. Then there are second levels of resource or timing issues including the following:

- Do you need to grow quickly because your company is experiencing a serious cash flow problem?

- Is there an opportunity that must be acted on quickly so you'll be able to reap the financial rewards?

Your Fiscal Vision is the Heart of Your Growth Strategy

The seriousness of the problem and the financial condition of your company will determine if your growth plan is a stop-gap measure to prevent the company from further hemorrhaging. Alternatively, your company may have the luxury of time and therefore may view a growth strategy as an opportunity in the offing that will help to strengthen your company's competitive position. Both scenarios, however, take into consideration your company's bottom line to determine the time frame in which you need to implement your strategy.

In recent years, one of the driving factors for a number of equity group controlled companies was the maturity of the fund and the liquidity demands of the limited partners. In some cases this allowed executing actions that were most beneficial for the long range, versus the quarter-to-quarter mentality that public companies must live with. For instance, a master franchisee/development company (discussed again in later chapters) was contractually required to develop 20 restaurants a year, or risk losing its franchise. Although it was 19 units behind schedule at the end of the first year, there was still time to solve problems with a longer range perspective than a public company might have had.

4. How are you going to fund at least the next two quarters?
Most CFOs will agree that it takes at least 6 months from the time a financing package is completed until the financing is available and in your bank. This is because (a) delays always happen, (b) a number of parties get involved, not the least of whom are several sets of attorneys, and (c) for your own particular reason, just think back to why your last financing was delayed. Usually in those cases where companies seem to obtain funding quicker than 6 months, someone was already working on the funding before the need was crucial. You may not have been involved or even aware of the ongoing process for the full 6 months, but, it was most likely there.

Executives tackling the funding question will often elicit some interesting and creative suggestions, from blue sky ideas to "that is a damn good idea" to "I never thought of that." Rest assured there are some innovative funding ideas out there -- 21 of which are included in Chapter 5, "Healthy Reserves: Cash Is King."

Of course, the funding question naturally raises other issues about the company's financial position. No matter how good an idea may be, if you don't have the financial resources to fund it, the idea isn't going to fly.

5. Where is your company financially?
If you don't know what your company's financial position is today (especially compared to your competition), you certainly won't be in a position to project how much money you'll need to grow your company in the future. Worse than that, you may be fooling yourself about the kind of risks you should and could take to grow the company. Ignoring a company's financial reality can have a devastating effect on a company's future. We need only look at today's global financial crisis to understand the enormity of this problem. When decision makers become so far removed from financial realities that they start to think projections have no bearing on outcomes, then you know financial disaster is about to strike. This funny money mentality is responsible for toppling whole industries, for example, housing, finance, insurance, and manufacturing — including the vaunted Big Three automakers.

Step 2: Follow-up Session

After you have discussed these issues and improved or created a fiscal vision, it's time to reconvene the executive team to answer another round of questions. These questions are designed to help you start relating your fiscal vision to your

Your Fiscal Vision is the Heart of Your Growth Strategy

growth strategy and will allow you to test your business model. (Think of testing the business model as relating the fiscal vision to the growth strategy.) Those of you who have participated in due diligence, operational reviews, or contingency planning will recognize aspects of the questions. Also, note that often this follow-up question/answer session draws out additional data or information that may lead you to modify your fiscal vision.

1. What are the three best longer-term opportunities you could create?

2. How can you best pursue those longer-term opportunities?

3. What are the top three risk concerns you have in meeting the current budget?

4. What actions can you take to minimize the risk of those concerns vis-à-vis the current budget?

5. What are the top three longer-term risk concerns the company faces and how would the company react if those concerns actually occurred?

6. What are the three most crucial infrastructure issues you face over the next one or two years?

These questions are formulated to create a laser focus on missed opportunities, gaps, or holes in the existing growth strategy or business plan. For example, if one or more of your best long-term opportunities are not in the current plan, growth in years two or three may suffer. Logically you would allocate some resources to begin exploring those opportunities. Conversely, if your Chief Operating Officer (COO) or Chief Financial Officer (CFO) doubts the company's ability to meet the current budget for one or more reasons he or she can communicate clearly, you should be concerned. Further, the one critical component of the

FiscalDoctor's approach that must be communicated clearly and effectively is that everyone must communicate clearly and effectively. Unspoken assumptions or misgivings going in to the fiscal vision, growth strategy or business plan will necessarily produce a flawed vision, strategy and plan coming out.

With each step and new set of questions, risks and concerns may be revealed that need to be incorporated into your fiscal vision and growth strategy. For instance, the process sometimes reveals that "we can stretch and obtain even more," while other times it reveals "we're betting the ranch" on a situation where reasonably accurate estimates of success do not make sense and a lesser goal, or creation of milestones toward that goal seem more appropriate. Identifying and developing your personal level of risk tolerance will be discussed in Chapter 3, and how your risk tolerance level impacts the company-wide enterprise risk management approach is discussed in Chapter 9, "When Bad Things Happen to Good Companies."

Step 3. Identify Resources Needed to Achieve Desired Outcome

Now you've gone through two rounds of questions and you should have a revised plan or more thoroughly vetted, realistic approach in hand. The discussion now turns to identifying the resources it will take to accomplish your goals.

Many of you will be reminded of situations in which either budgets or business plans were developed and driven from the "top-down" with no consideration given to the personnel, money, facilities, or outside resources needed to meet the stated goals. Allowing the various departments to draw up their budgets and goals to meet the company's overall growth strategy dramatically improves the accuracy of the business model and generates needed buy-in from the people who will execute the vision. Some readers may question how to handle the problem that some department heads inflate resources needed or are overly conservative about obtainable results. The process of balancing "top-down" plans that are sometimes insensitive to reality and "bottom-up" plans that are sometimes self-serving should decrease dramatically after the first year of the budgeting process. When budget discussions stall, it usually signals problems within the organization's culture, including leadership or incentive plan issues. (These problems go beyond the concerns of this book.)

Regardless of how thorough your business plans or projections are, it is always important to review the six follow-up questions in Step 2. In fact, as part of the process, I often work with additional members of the executive team to help them develop a single business wide enterprise risk management framework, which can then be used in all future planning.

Step 4. Validate the Viability of Your Business Model

It goes without saying that your fiscal vision needs to support your business model and revenue assumptions. Otherwise, not only will your growth strategy fail, but your entire company may be in serious danger of failing. You need to be able to answer some fundamental questions like, "Can we really sell that many units at those prices without jeopardizing our customer base?" Integral to this process is the fact that most high-growth companies already have in place a viable business model. Sometimes you just need a second opinion on how to improve or accelerate results under that model, and the prior steps can be used to generate that second look. However, when something in this process or an external event causes a decision maker or its team to suspect that the business model needs something more than tweaking, we stop and take the time to review the plan and its underlying assumptions. This step either is quickly resolved or becomes a deeper issue as discussed in Chapter 6, "How Fit Is Your Business Model?"

Step 5: Obtain the Data the Team Needs

Throughout the whole process you may need to obtain additional data in order for the team to make informed decisions. The need for further information can occur almost anywhere in the process—from the key decision maker who wants to think more about soft issues such as why the executive team should be committed to this company or product to the management team's need for more data before it is comfortable with attaining budgets or validating the business model. If you think more data will help your decision-making process, now is a good time to seek out that information. We will talk about this in more detail in Chapter 8, "Stress-Test: Show Me the Data (on Time!)."

 ### Coming Up

In the next chapter, we'll talk more about acknowledging your appetite for risk and how your risk tolerance impacts your company. At the end of the chapter, you will be in a better position to optimize your opportunities, increase your revenue, maximize your profits, and grow your company to meet your goals.

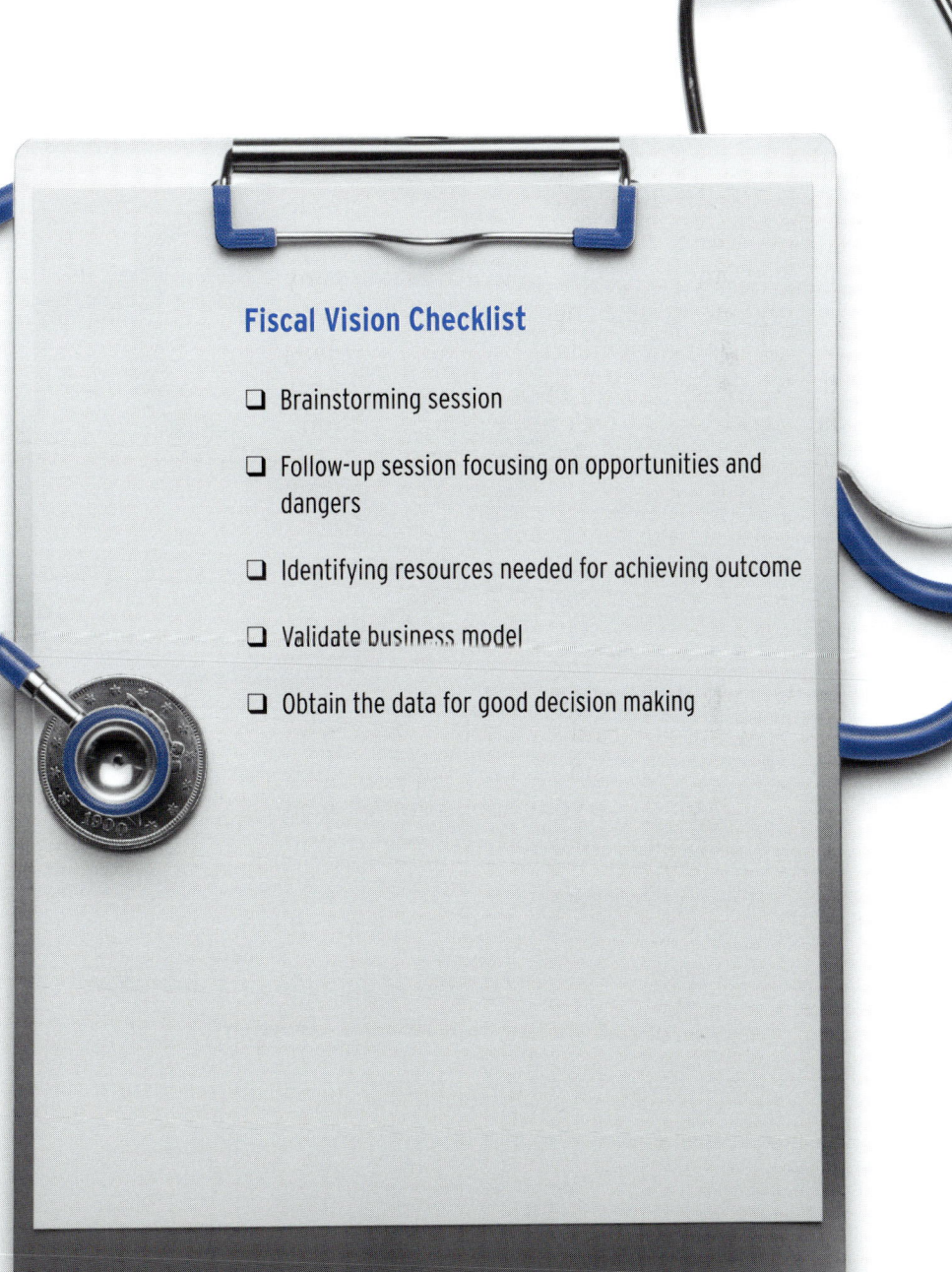

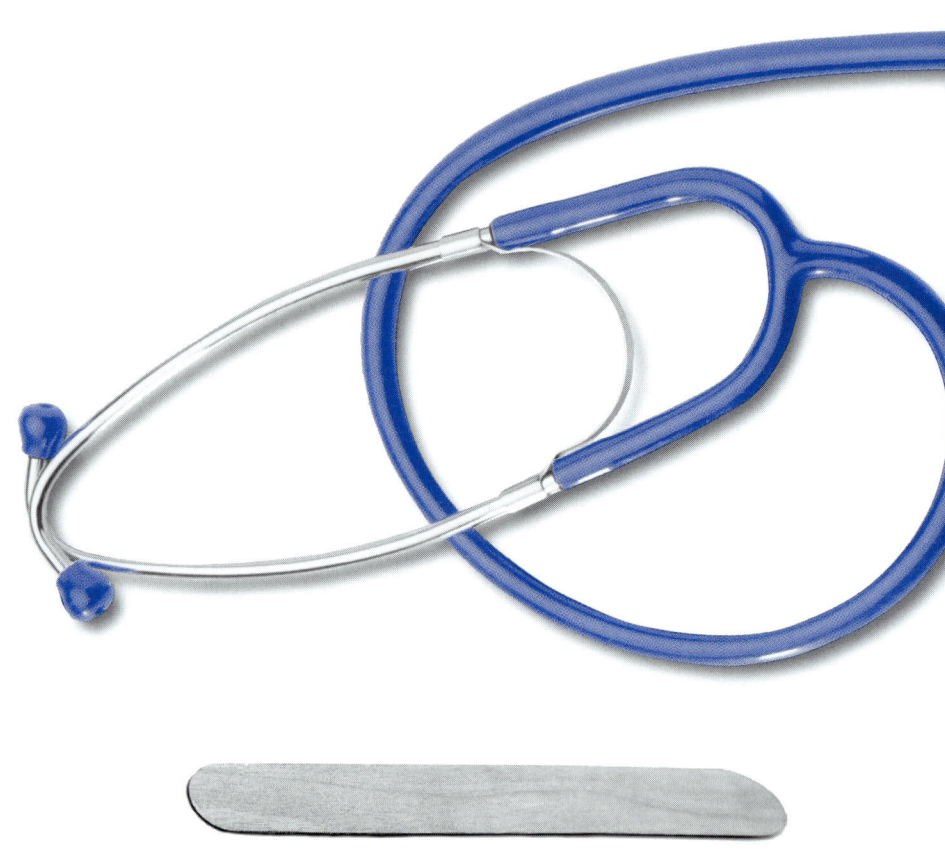

Security is mostly a superstition. It does not exist in nature, nor do the children of men as a whole experience it. Avoiding danger is no safer in the long run than outright exposure. Life is either a daring adventure or nothing.

–Hellen Keller

What Is Your Appetite for Risk?

Investopedia defines risk tolerance as "the degree of uncertainty that an investor can handle in regard to a negative change in the value of his or her portfolio." On a scale from 1 to 10, there are some small business owners who view risk exposure as an issue warranting scant analysis (1 on the scale) to large companies that spend millions on very precise, sophisticated analysis (10 on the scale).

Regardless of whether you're on the low or high end, most people will agree that there are two types of risk companies (of all sizes) face:

1. Taking a risk or not taking a risk *to reap a potential reward.*

2. Taking a risk or not taking a risk *to prevent a negative outcome from occurring.*

The scenarios below, while simplistic, provide a basic overview (or a review) of the psychology of Risk Tolerance 101. For the sake of this discussion, let's use the idea of a coin toss with a friend to see where you naturally fall on the risk tolerance scale. I recommend doing this simple exercise before moving to the seriousness of "risk taking" as it pertains to your company.

○ You put up $1,000 to your friend's $1,500. Winner takes all.

○ You put up $10,000 to your friend's $20,000. Winner takes all.

○ You put up $100,000 to your friend's $250,000. Winner takes all.

Most people drop out fairly quickly on this progression even though the odds are getting better to win. This means that for an event with an equal chance to win or lose, your potential winnings per dollar invested increases from $1.50 to $2.00 and even to $2.50. Why drop out as each dollar bet gets the chance for even better returns? The reason? The cost of losing gets too high, as your $1,000 bet accelerates to $10,000 and then $100,000, while you have no ability to improve your likelihood of winning above the original even odds. (Resource 3 in the Resources Section of this book contains more quantitative comments on risk tolerance.)

To drive home the point about different risk tolerance personalities, consider the Monster.com Super Bowl ad. Many leaders would be hesitant to bet everything on one event even if they carefully evaluated the situation and their team had done everything possible to reduce the chances of failure. But that wasn't the case for this entrepreneurial CEO. In 1999, Monster.com CEO Jeff Taylor spent $4 million for three 30-second TV ads on the Super Bowl for his internet job-search business. (You can see the ad on YouTube.)

What many people did not know or have forgotten is that the bet was actually $700,000 higher: Monster.com purchased $700,000 of new network Dell servers and a T-3 pipe to support the response they expected, and received. Taylor remarked, "At 10:30 p.m. or 11 p.m., after the Super Bowl was over, we were doing almost 2,900 job searches per minute. That spike leveled off to 1,500 later in the week, still 400 per minute more than the pre-Super Bowl high."

CNN.com featured an article describing in detail the technical factors and comparing this to other companies that did NOT have the supporting infrastructure in place to handle success. A number of you may remember stories of other companies that made a similar bet and lost big time either because the action did not have a payback, or they did not plan well enough to hedge the risks related to their company's strategy.

It goes without saying that at the heart of every risk management strategy is a contingency plan that serves as a backup (a.k.a. a safety net) in the event that the risk strategy goes awry, or worse, Murphy's Law comes into effect. In fact, building a contingency plan into an organization's culture is *de rigueur* for the long-term health of a company. Chapter 9, "ER: When Bad Things Happen to Good Companies," will go into more detail about contingency planning.

The Framework: Five Crucial Questions

Before a decision maker and executive team begin putting flesh on the bones of a risk management strategy, they need to address the following five questions to determine their personal risk tolerance levels. The answers to these questions will be the driving factors that help the team create a risk management strategy they are all comfortable supporting.

1. How risk tolerant are you, your board of directors, and your executive team?

2. How complete and accurate is the financial information you currently have to make the decision you are contemplating?

3. What is the worst-case scenario that can happen if you do or don't act? This is where your personal "contingency plan" comes into play.

4. How committed are you, your executive team, and your board of directors to executing the risk strategy?

5. What issues are potential doomsday scenarios for your company? For example, what is the impact of acting and failing, or failing to act to suffer the consequences?

1. How risk tolerant are you?

On the surface, it appears that this question revolves around the age and history of the company. (Lurking just below the surface are other critical concerns like the amount of money involved versus cash balances, your ownership percentage in the company, the industry you are in, stage of corporate life, or compensation).

For example, conventional thinking would conclude that a younger company has a higher level of risk tolerance than an older, more established company. However, an established company may have a high risk tolerance because it has gained deep industry knowledge, competitive advantage, strong financial resources, and expertise that put it in a favorable position to take risks.

That said, the real test of a company's risk tolerance, whether you run a young or a more established business, comes down to one simple fact: You and your executive team must have the courage and ability not only to acknowledge when your risk tolerance has changed (for better or for worse; from high to low) but more important to change or alter your risk strategy in midstream. In this case, you need to be able to make the necessary adjustments and review your risk analysis strategy until your overall game plan and the efforts required are achievable to realize your desired outcome.

After you have determined the amount of risk you are willing to take for the targeted rewards (your goals vis-à-vis your risk tolerance), you are ready to create a framework for future decisions and a schedule to identify those risks you are willing to take. In fact, by doing this, you may find your goals can be reasonably reached without incurring as much risk as you previously thought. The real goal here is to minimize risk while reaching or exceeding your business objectives.

2. *How complete and accurate is the financial information you currently have to make your decision?*
This question can't be answered until you've answered an attendant question: "When does the risk decision need to be made?" Today? Tomorrow? Six months from now? There is a substantial amount of financial information available to support your decision-making process. (Go to Resource 1 for a list.)

If you are not sure whether your answer is that you do or do not have complete and adequate information available, there is an easy way to find out:

- Identify a low-likelihood risk, issue X, for which no plan exists and, which if it occurred, would require a very rapid response;

- Select someone who does not normally work in that area to resolve the issue within an estimated deadline;

- When that person goes through the process of having to solve issue X on a short time frame with inadequate information, the impact of manual work-arounds, etc., will instantly show up. And let's be truthful here, you probably were generous and optimistic about the length of time you estimated to solve issue X.

Executing this process will start improving available financial information completeness and accuracy.

Some people may then ask, "How do we know when we have enough timely usable information?" There is a simple answer that many executives have given me—when you've got the key items you need to run your business and the information is robust enough for you to "sleep better at night."

Those key items include:

- One-page summary of the balance sheet with the five key operating and financial issues, or key metrics, operations uses to run the business (This is sometimes called a Flash Report when the report is also used to quickly provide feedback on key issues. Resource 2 has an example of a Flash Report.) This requires the company to determine and agree on what really matters, from the perspective of the operational people who actually run the business and execute the corporate strategy.

- One-page summary of the income statement categories with a comparison to budget and notes on any meaningful variances. Far too many information systems drown management teams with reams of data, obscuring their ability to focus on information that really matters. The one-page formats suggested here and in the preceding step spotlight key trend or issues, with the capability to provide extensive detail when asked.

- Oral update of no more than a one-page recap on key points that should be emphasized across departments, such as a reference to sales or business development on major prospective bookings, key staffing needs, or potential debt violations.

Often the hardest parts of the package are determining what the crucial business metrics are, agreeing on how timely information is needed, or focusing executive attention on the really meaningful information. (This may sound obvious, but because it's hard, many companies could do a much better job on at least one of these three issues.)

3. *What is the worst-case scenario if you do or don't act?*
I'm amazed by how few companies have a contingency plan that takes a worst-case scenario into consideration. This is too bad because I can't emphasize enough what the unintended psychological benefits can be when you create a contingency plan that has a worst-case scenario component. Somehow the practice of planning for a worst-case situation in and of itself better prepares the company to execute a contingency plan when and if the time comes to do so. It's the same psychology that we use to prepare our troops for war: The better we train our soldiers to fight under the worst conditions, the better equipped they are to fight under any condition. Being prepared is the key.

4. *How committed are you, your executive team and your board of directors to creating and executing the risk strategy?*
The work to define and acknowledge your risk tolerance is like taking vitamin supplements or a flu shot; it's a preventative measure that you take so you won't get "sick." Talking about your risk tolerance may not be a pleasant discussion, and it's a discussion that many executive teams would like to dismiss or put on the back burner, but the sooner you come to terms with your risk tolerance, the better off you'll be financially. You and your team should acknowledge that as the final decision makers, the overriding factor that will determine the success or failure of your risk strategy is your commitment to creating the risk strategy in the first place, and if need be, to executing it.

As I mentioned, I am always surprised by how few companies create worst-case contingency plans. It's always disheartening to learn the extent to which a risk management mindset does not prevail in corporate America. In 2006, the *Journal of Accountancy* (December 2006) published the results of a risk management survey in a report, "The Best Laid Plans." The survey stated that while 90% of executives said they wanted to build an ERM process into their organizations, only 11% had completed the implementation. (The source of the survey: The Conference Board with responses from 271 risk management executives.) Often companies want to start at too high a level of sophistication and quit because of the challenges. They would benefit from just starting and getting something in place. The strategy can always be improved over time.

5. *What issues are potential doomsday scenarios for your company?*

Let's define a doomsday scenario as a catastrophic event that could destroy you or your company. Even if the likelihood of this to occur was very low, most management teams would certainly make a concerted effort to prevent the disaster from occurring. This is why insurance companies reinsure risks, so when a Class 5 hurricane hits costing billions of dollars, the insurance company is not bankrupted. Also think of how major risks turned out for Fannie Mae, Lehman Brothers, Bear Sterns, or AIG. You have to be able to draw lines in the sand and say that you will not exceed certain issues and not take on certain risks. As John Wayne would say, "Don't bet the ranch."

It is a shame when an external risk you could not reasonably anticipate dramatically impacts your company. It is even worse when a risk dramatically impacts your company that you *should have anticipated* with some serious strategic and contingency planning. So invest some of strategic planning time to think about how you will recognize special situations that, although unlikely, would be catastrophic for you or your company?

For instance, why were so many suppliers to the automotive industry caught so ill prepared for the likelihood of at least one of the Big 3 — Ford, GM or Chrysler — either going bankrupt or dramatically changing economic models? Experts reporting that the companies were actually bankrupt or insolvent were ignored for years. Still, many suppliers ignored the warning signs and kept doing business as usual with no contingency plans for the looming catastrophe.

Some of you should also include a less dramatic issue in this final self-analysis step, namely, how do you recognize when there are cash flow issues that prevent pursuing an option even if it fits within your risk tolerance? This will be especially pertinent over the next few years for those with access to cash because there will be numerous opportunities. Some of you may be thinking, *just give me a simple and preferably less painful example of a risk tolerance I can relate to*. One of my clients had a risk tolerance that related to cash. His idea of risk was, "So long as we have $800,000 cash in the bank, I sleep well at night. Tell me when we get below that level." His rationale for that number included having enough money to cover salaries and basic operating expenses coverage to provide time to adapt to an unusual event. If you or a member of your team has made similar statements, you, indeed, have determined your risk tolerance.

The Bottom Line

The nature of disasters and catastrophes are that they happen when we least expect them. Therefore, it is critical that you calibrate where your risk tolerance is today. Don't wait until some major event occurs when you will have to make a decision with less information than you desire in a shorter time frame than you think is fair, with much more at stake than you normally feel comfortable about.

Coming Up

In Chapter 4 we hunker down to discuss common areas where bottom line dollars may be gained or lost as you move toward corporate fiscal well-being. We will also examine ways to continue improving the health of your business by gaining a better understanding of sales and operating information as well as how to avoid the dreaded cash flow crunch.

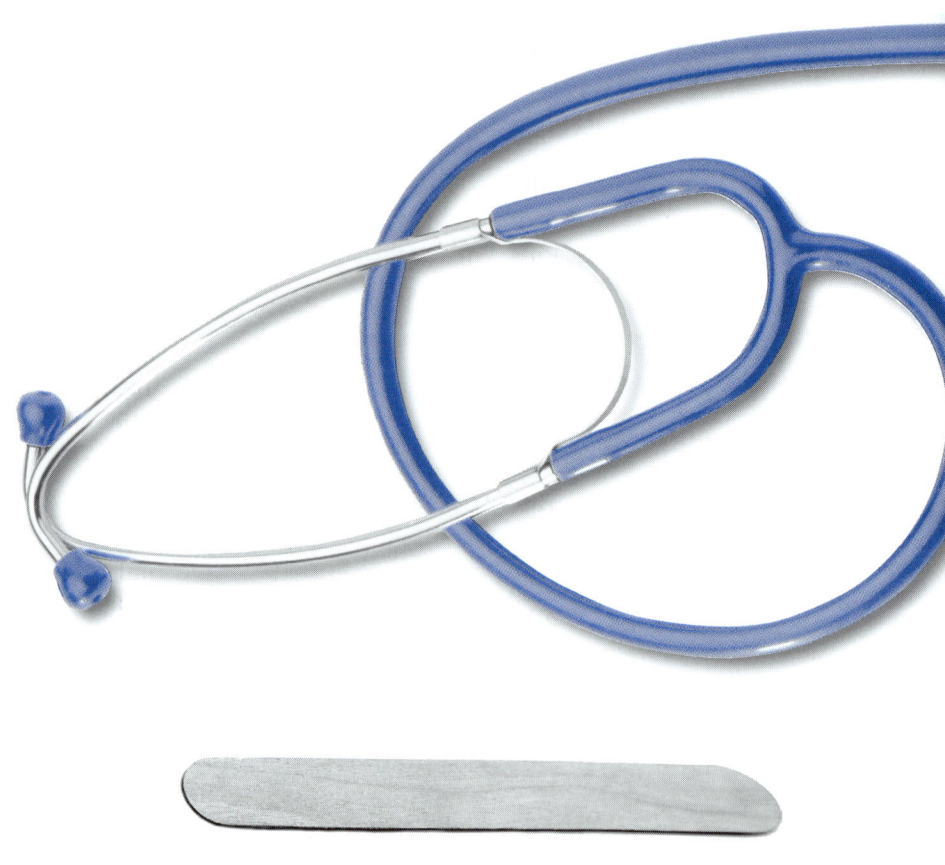

*The greatest obstacle to discovery is not ignorance—
it is the illusion of knowledge.*

−Daniel Boorstin

The Internal Exam: Five Areas Where Risk Can Lurk

While numbers in and of themselves are neutral, the way they are interpreted can be misleading. According to a 2002 *Electronic Business* article, "A full 17% of respondents admitted that their CEOs had pressured them to misrepresent results at least once."

Without pointing fingers, could your financial statements, projections, and results use a more accurate interpretation? Besides giving you a more accurate picture of your company's financial fitness, an accurate understanding will have a major side benefit over the next year. The better you understand your company's real position, the more accurate the information will be that you depend upon to run your business. Depending upon how they are treated at your company, I've identified five areas that can either provide strategic benefits going forward if corrected, or be landmines where risk may be lurking in your company, if ignored. Let's make lemonade from lemons, if any of these issues still exist at your company.

How does your company stack up to these statements?

1. My business does not accurately know who its 10 most profitable customers are.

    ○ True   ○ False

2. Occasionally my business capitalized expenses that created an asset with what now may be a questionable recorded value.

    ○ True   ○ False

3. My company does not know how changes at one of our top 10 customers may affect our company's bottom line.

○ True   ○ False

4. My business has an asset it would be better off selling at a loss to free up cash to pursue a more promising opportunity.

○ True   ○ False

5. My business paints an overly optimistic picture of our company to a customer, vendor, or financing source.

○ True   ○ False

1. The Value of Knowing Your Most Profitable Customers

How many times have you asked or been asked some version of this question: *If you find out who our 10 most profitable customers are, could you please let me know?* I can't tell you how many times I've heard top executives ask this question. Like a well-kept family secret, companies often can't accurately identify their 10 most profitable customers. Some companies may define their top 10 customers in terms of those with the largest revenue. At some point in the company's history that might have been a reasonable approach. In this case, there are reasonable time frames when the product line does not have to be very wide, customer service issues may be minor, margin erosion has not begun, and even costs of production are reasonably stable.

However, as your business becomes more complicated or more competitive requiring new or more modern software programs and/or incompatible record keeping systems, the business may not have the money to immediately upgrade information systems and must get by for now with what they have. In those cases, I've found that accurately knowing the 10 most profitable

The Internal Exam: Five Areas Where Risk Can Lurk

customers means digging a little deeper to get a better understanding of the numbers.

For example, I once worked with a steel company that had invested in software and hardware systems that could handle high volume manufacturing of a limited number of products with a limited choice of options. When the industry became much more competitive, customers demanded a wider range of customized product options, including color, length, and width. The more competitive environment meant they needed better operating information to become more cost effective while still meeting new and wider customer demands.

The information systems that worked well in the past could not meet these new customer demands. The company had not funded investment in new manufacturing systems or new data systems. Normally inside such companies, people solve these problems with unofficial Excel spreadsheets. Excel's flexibility solves the lack of flexibility inside the official system. After all, customers want their product delivered their way, how they need it, and when they need it, and do not care how the company's internal information system works.

However, even if the accounting department can deliver the financial statements and reports required by the SEC, management must have the right information to run the business successfully. If this is "offline" in a spreadsheet on a manager's laptop instead of in "the system," the information may not be easily accessible or in a format that is easily usable. Or it may take time and energy to integrate the spreadsheet data with the "online system" data. (Think of the last discussion or meeting you attended where a manager insisted they he or she couldn't get the information he or she was requesting.) Whatever the situation, there are clearly more costs associated with both providing the customized services to the client and accessing and presenting the data for management.

Often, the short-term answer is to throw bodies at the problem. Sometimes the mid-range solution is to get the right eight people in a room for a day and see what information is needed and how it can be delivered. That can initiate the process to obtain needed information and help clear red tape for management and their teams. Whatever level of access to this information your company has, I strongly recommend regularly obtaining the information about your most profitable customers. We will examine this issue in more detail later in this chapter. After all, you would be hard pressed to find anyone who disagrees with the statement that customers are the lifeblood of his or her business.

2. Question Today the Ongoing Value of Capitalized Items

Would you feel better about the issue of capitalization if you saw examples of how large companies with access to award-winning systems still make monumental mistakes when they misread the market? For example, Cisco had world-class information systems and processes for financial reporting and operational controls in place when it wrote off $3 billion of inventory in 2001. In a series of widely discussed articles about how a write-off of such magnitude could occur with a company that has such sophisticated systems, Cisco's executives admitted they misread the market downturn. At least Cisco made an honest, but embarrassing, mistake, but I wonder how many other companies would openly acknowledge such an error.

Another example is Fannie Mae. In business parlance, what Fannie Mae did is sometimes called "cooking the books" — not a good thing to do. Fannie Mae made highly questionable valuation decisions, not just once but twice. But the clean up team who was brought in to right the wrong appears to have made even more expensive and questionable actions than the "bad" people they had replaced. Possibly, the motives of the second team were less questionable than the motives of the first team and were closer to reckless risk taking than unethical behavior. Nonetheless, the net result was that in November 2008, Fannie Mae indicated that it would write off $20 billion in tax-related assets.

While it may be several years before we have better indications of the total costs to shareholders and taxpayers of today's financial institutions' failures to make tough decisions, we never will know the real total cost of these wrongdoings. Companies of all sizes have legitimately capitalized some item in the past that should be regularly questioned. All of us have read the horror stories of write-offs that in hindsight raise questions that often were not valid or even a factor when they originated.

If you have reserves, allowances or estimates for loss, it is a worthwhile hedge against downside risk to take a more critical look at them now and at least once a year going forward. When bad things happen to good companies, some of the reasons those things were not corrected earlier can be tremendously embarrassing later, when the bad things are on the front page of the *Wall Street Journal*. Why do you think incoming presidents of turnaround situations scrutinize everything and clean house–sometimes referred to as writing off everything including the kitchen sink? They would rather embarrass the outgoing leader than be the subject of embarrassment in the future.

3. Analyze Your Top Ten Customers' Profits

Companies that accurately know the profitability of sales of their top 10 customers often fail to surmount the next hurdle: *How will your company be affected when the profitability of your top customer decreases?* There is always a time when one of your top 10 customers will drop off your "A list." Consider that buggy whip manufacturers were profitable customers for some businesses until automobiles became the standard. Rather than laugh at that comparison, review how the product or service your company provides might become the buggy whip of tomorrow for one or more of your current best customers.

Even if you know your 10 most profitable customers, you still can be caught unaware if you do not have some understanding of how changes in your customers' business will impact your business. A company that has no clue who its most profitable customers are cannot even begin to estimate the damaging impact on their own company when their top customers' profits decline. The takeaway lesson here is to understand that your top 10 customers will change over time, so it's up to your management team to continuously analyze customer data to ensure you're serving the *right 10* best customers at all times and recognize that adjustments need to be made to those customer accounts that have fallen off the A list.

4. The Company Would Be Better Off Selling the Asset

Has your CEO, CFO, or financial department ever mentioned that the company has to keep losing money on a branch, service, or product because it can't afford the financial loss it would have to record to dispose of the asset? I've been privy to such discussions many times in corporations of all sizes. What happened to companies in those circumstances is that they either did not fully understand the real value of their assets, or they chose to look at their assets through rose-colored glasses.

A smaller-scale version of this situation occurs when a business fails to look at return on equity related to assets or departments. Many companies have one or more assets that can be associated with a band-aid solution, or assets that should be sold (even at a loss) and reinvested in another opportunity. This can be particularly true when the executive bonuses are mainly a function of the absolute dollar level of profitability, with limited influence from return on equity or similar measurements.

The Internal Exam: Five Areas Where Risk Can Lurk

Let's use our "magic decoder ring" on a statement all too often heard. You (another person or company) would be better off selling stock, the asset, or even in some cases, the company, and just putting the money in treasury bills. In fact, I know of a situation where the subsidiaries of a holding company earned 2% on equity when the prime rate was 4%.

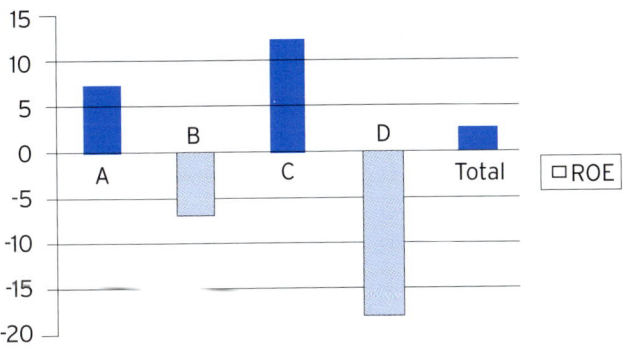

Return on Equity % by Subsidiary and In Total

Company X	ROE
A	7.5
B	-7.0
C	12.5
D	-18.0
Total	**2.5**

After viewing the chart, compare your business. Then ask, *What situation or valuation in our company are we looking at through rose-colored glasses?* A similar area where you might look for the rose-colored glasses within your company is your capital expenditures program (CAPEX). For those of you who are saying your company has a mechanism that investment proposals meet threshold rates, how often does someone report back convincingly that the actual investment return met or exceeded the level projected to get the funding? I suspect the answer is not as often as you think!

5. My Business Paints an Overly Optimistic Picture to Our Customers, Vendors or Finance Sources

How many companies have painted an overly optimistic picture to a customer, vendor, or financing source? According to *ADP Screening and Selection Services* "44% of Americans lie about their work history." (One well-publicized example was the case of Marilee Jones, who was the admissions director at Massachusetts Institute of Technology. While she claimed to have degrees from Albany Medical College, Union College and Rensselaer Polytechnic Institute, it turned out that she falsified her academic degrees: She had no degrees from any of them.) If any of those 44% work at your company, might they stretch the truth a little while representing your company?

The effects of this are extremely hard to quantify. When does puffery become misrepresentation? Murphy's Law suggests not knowing your company's real equity and risk areas will be a problem at the most inopportune time. Just take a look at all the items someone like me will ask for during a due diligence process and follow-up to see if your company's rough areas remain hidden. Also, if the numbers are clear, then it's more difficult to misrepresent them — whether intentionally or not.

 ## Coming Up

In the next chapter, we will take a closer look at decision makers' number one obsession — access to cash.

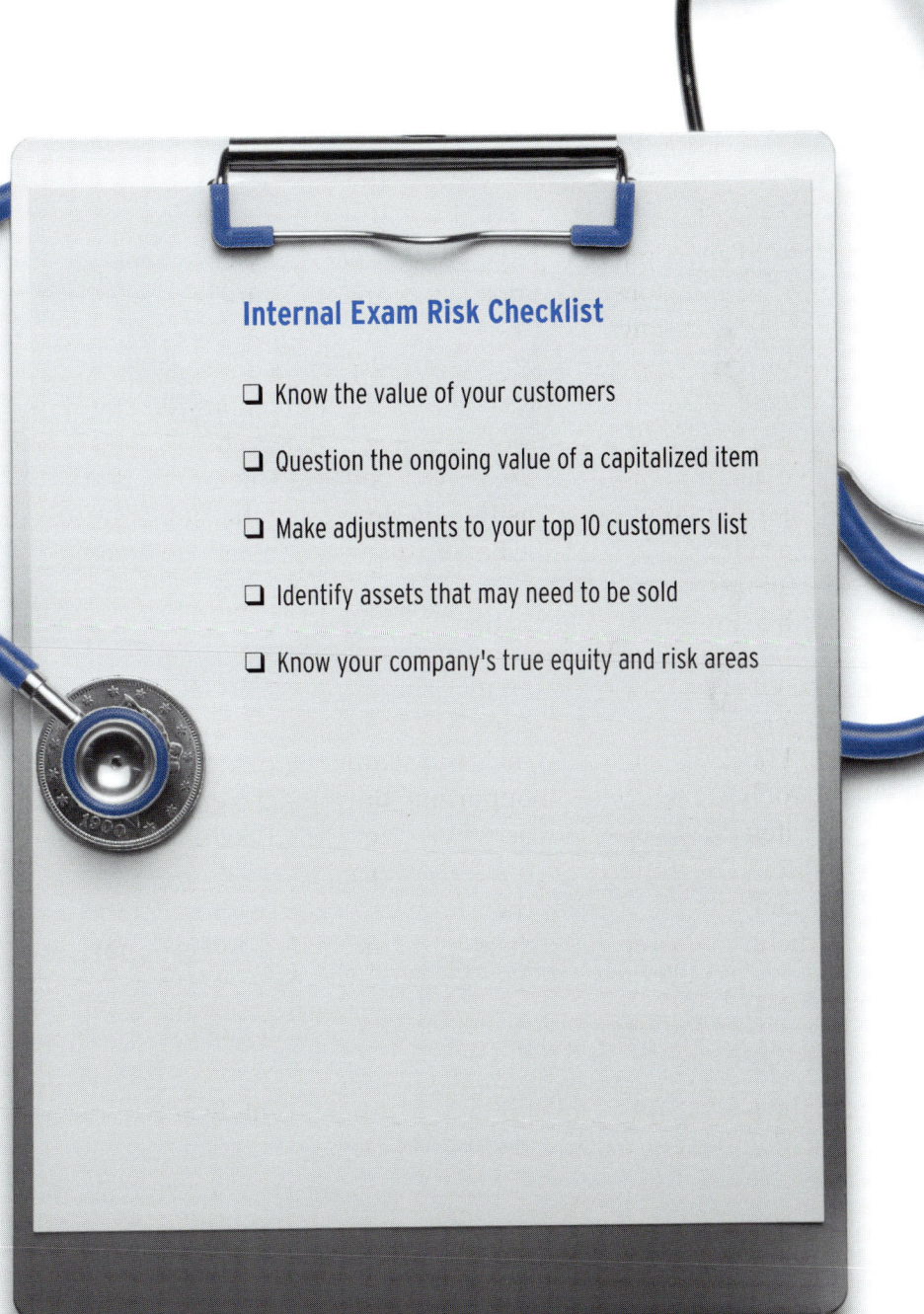

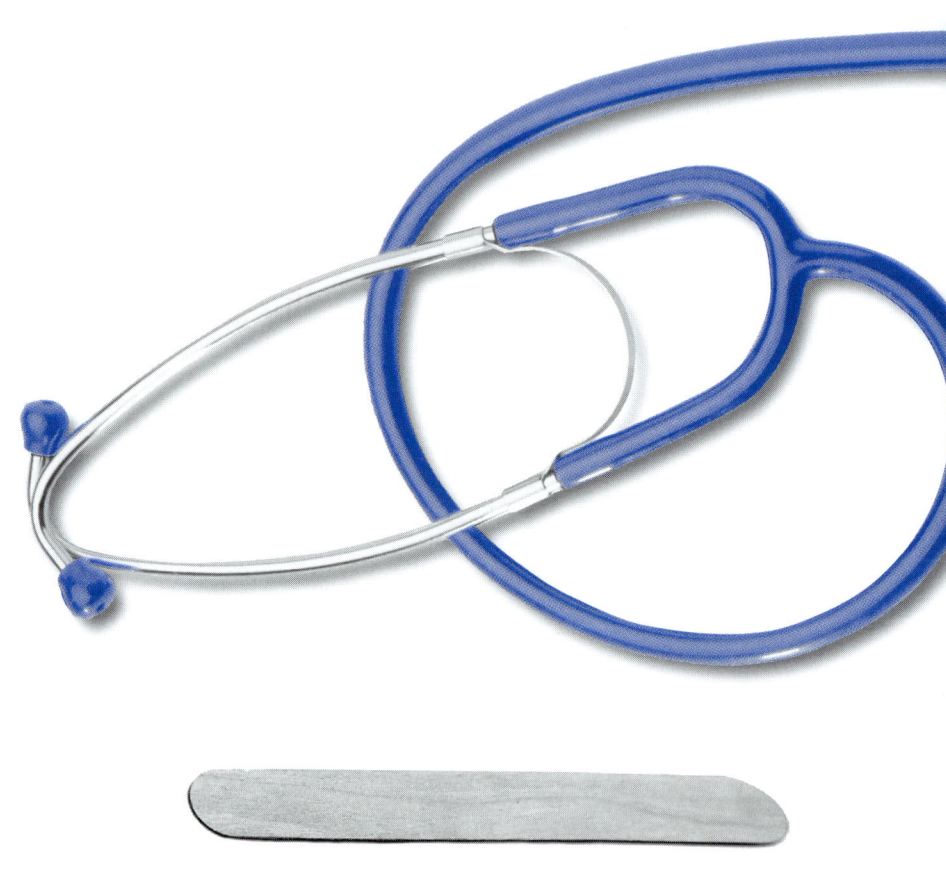

You have reached the pinnacle of success as soon as you become uninterested in money, compliments, or publicity.

–Thomas Wolfe

Healthy Reserves: Why Cash Is King

In light of the recent collapse of our financial and banking institutions, few will dispute the critical importance of having a nice padding of good old-fashioned cash. In fact, if ever there was a time when a healthy reserve of cash is required, it's now. When considering your cash position, think about these scenarios:

○ Otherwise successful/promising companies running out of cash

○ Additional financing costs of having a poor cash position

○ Inability to handle unforeseen risks or exploit opportunities

○ Distraction caused by crisis management

What Is a Reasonable Cash Flow Reserve?

One of the first questions I ask CEOs is, "How much cash do you need to sleep well at night?" Typically the answer is a minimum of 1 month's operating expenses. Often the CEOs I speak with want enough cash to pay 3 months' salaries. The point being that with that amount in reserve, they can focus on other important issues as long as there are no major cash expenditures projected. There is a popular story about how Bill Gates wanted at least 6 months' available cash when he was building Microsoft.

Behind the rationale of cash reserve is an understanding of how long it takes to convert assets to cash. Young companies should plan for 6 to 8 months from when an investor package is deemed complete to the funding (when the check actually clears the bank). Later stage companies with a good earnings history and reliable and loyal customers may need substantially less time if they have strong banking relationships and have kept their financing sources well-informed of their financial condition.

What Forms Can Cash Take?

Most executives don't want to spend half their time raising cash and half their time living in crisis mode. Since it normally does not make sense to have excessive amounts of cash sitting in a bank account, the conversation turns to *what items are (almost) as good as cash*? Profitable customers paying within reasonable time frames will always be the preferred cash source. Sweep accounts, money market accounts, and marketable securities also earn interest income while still providing almost immediate access to cash. Bankers will be glad to discuss their latest versions of standby lines of credit, asset-based loans and factoring. Listen carefully as costs and personal guarantees vary dramatically, and you don't want to be learning about this process when you have little or no time to understand your options.

How Can You Make Better Cash Flow Projections?

Some CFOs — often to the frustration of their CEOs — make the cash projection process seem much harder than it needs to be, and then they use the difficulty argument as an excuse to do minimal or no cash planning. I've heard countless stories of $100 million plus companies having minimal or no cash planning process. My recommendation is to just get started somewhere and track it against actual performance to adjust it to become more accurate and build confidence in the future. At a minimum, any company that is in growth mode should start with broad projections of cash receipts and disbursements by major categories, such as collections of receivables, payroll, vendor payments, and regularly scheduled debt or lease payments.

As you begin to develop a projection history, which should include finding reasonable ways to obtain relevant information, you should make the process more detailed by either moving to biweekly or weekly time periods or developing more specific projected cash categories. This requires patience. I recall a situation where I created basic monthly cash flow projections for a company where none previously existed. Instead of testing the system or even asking for weekly projections, the company immediately wanted me to improve the rough projections to predict not just the month the company would run out of money but the day of the week!

How Do Cash Flow Projections Improve Planning?

Most CEOs will say the value of a business plan is that it helps management focus on the company vision, action plans, and resources needed to meet corporate goals for the time frame covered, usually at least the next year. They also will say that somehow it always seems easier to accurately project spending money than project collecting money. It seems like everyone can make their cost budget but very few meet the income budget.

Business plans that don't include cash projections are harder to execute whenever unexpected opportunities or difficulties occur. For example, substantial growth, new product offerings, or building infrastructure often requires the ability to rapidly commit and spend money. A company that is ill prepared to pursue funding may be forced to guesstimate key operating assumptions such as how long it takes newly hired salespeople to meet their sales quotas. I've witnessed bankers embarrass CEOs when they raise this very question, but it seems some CEOs just don't to have a good answer. Don't be one of those CEOs—have the information ready before you need it.

How Long a Time Frame Should Projections Cover?

This may fly in the face of Thomas Friedman's worldview as expressed in *The World Is Flat*, but I contend that five-year projections are still relevant, and in some cases absolutely necessary. To this point, the first year will always be more detailed than subsequent years: In fact, by year five, the assumptions may be considerably less detailed and may only serve an inspirational purpose. But that doesn't make that fifth year any less important.

For example, a five-year projection may be required when a board of directors or prospective investors want to see a well-articulated vision and a detailed strategy for multiple years to gain an understanding of how the company expects to grow a business opportunity to the $100 million level. At the very least, a company should have at least monthly projections for the next 12 to 24 months on some rolling basis. After that, year three may have quarterly or annual projections: Years four and five may just have annual projections. Remember, it's not set in stone. Markets change, the economic climate changes, and your projections will change. But at least you have some projections at the ready.

For those who now see the usefulness of cash projections, you're ready to consider some of the suggestions described above. For those who still aren't convinced of the need for cash projections, may I remind you that when a cash crunch does occur (as we're living through today), top management typically is the last salaried personnel to be paid? Is this how you want to run your company? I think not. For those who would settle for a way to stretch out operations while they improve cash projections or raise money, the next section is for you.

21 Ways to Generate Quick Cash

Many of the practices below should be ones you're already doing on a consistent basis. While some of these items may not apply to your business or cannot be done within 60 days, the sooner you put into practice those that are pertinent, the sooner you can reap the financial rewards and improve your cash flow.

1. Send out all accounts receivable statements monthly.

2. Increase your cash discount for prompt payment.

3. Call customers who owe you money and ask for payment. Be sure to include monthly interest charges of 1.5 % of past due portion.

4. Sell slower moving inventory at a discount. Better yet, try sending your inventory back to the manufacturer for credit. Who knows, the manufacturer may need it for another customer.

5. Review inventory levels by how many day's sales and adjust outstanding and future orders appropriately.

6. Sell and lease back assets.

7. Increase your line of credit.

8. Review intellectual property for royalty opportunities.

9. Review staffing levels and staff on a "green field" basis. Ask yourself the following questions: If you were starting a new company, would you hire the employees you have today? If you would hire them, would you have them in the positions they are in today?

10. Learn which products are loss leaders and either get rid of them or, at the very least, consider raising prices.

11. Raise prices where appropriate on any product or service.

12. Find ways to reduce scrap.

13. Ask employees for suggestions. An adage comes to mind: "Ain't any of us as smart as all of us."

14. Slow vendor payments temporarily.

15. Postpone purchases.

16. Review your controls over these two areas: (a) question why your legal and professional bills are so high; (b) reduce advertising budget and instead increase your public relations efforts.

17. Review the rest of your expenses on a line-by-line basis.

18. Assign customer write-offs to a collection agency.

19. Speed up customer invoicing time frame.

20. Operate on a pro-forma basis. Don't extend credit to your customers.

21. Do more with less. There is a reason why this tried-and-true phrase exists.

Even better than thinking in crisis mode, why not think strategically about your company's cash flow before a cash crunch becomes a critical problem that could endanger the growth, or worse, the survival of your company. In fact, I recommend pulling this list out every six months to see where and how you can better manage your company's cash flow. When the economic climate changes as dramatically and as frequently as it seems to be nowadays, remember that cash is king more than ever.

While this checklist is a handy guide to improve your infrastructure and accelerate cash flow, I can't stress enough the point I make throughout this book. Pay attention to your number one cash generator: *your most profitable customers*. To this point, perhaps it's time to consider the 80/20 rule. Do business with those 20% of your customers that give you 80% of your business.

Resource 4 contains a brief overall summary of the various accounting resource levels and functions of a CFO and a controller.

Coming Up

In the next chapter we'll take a look at some methods of strategic planning to help improve the health of your business model.

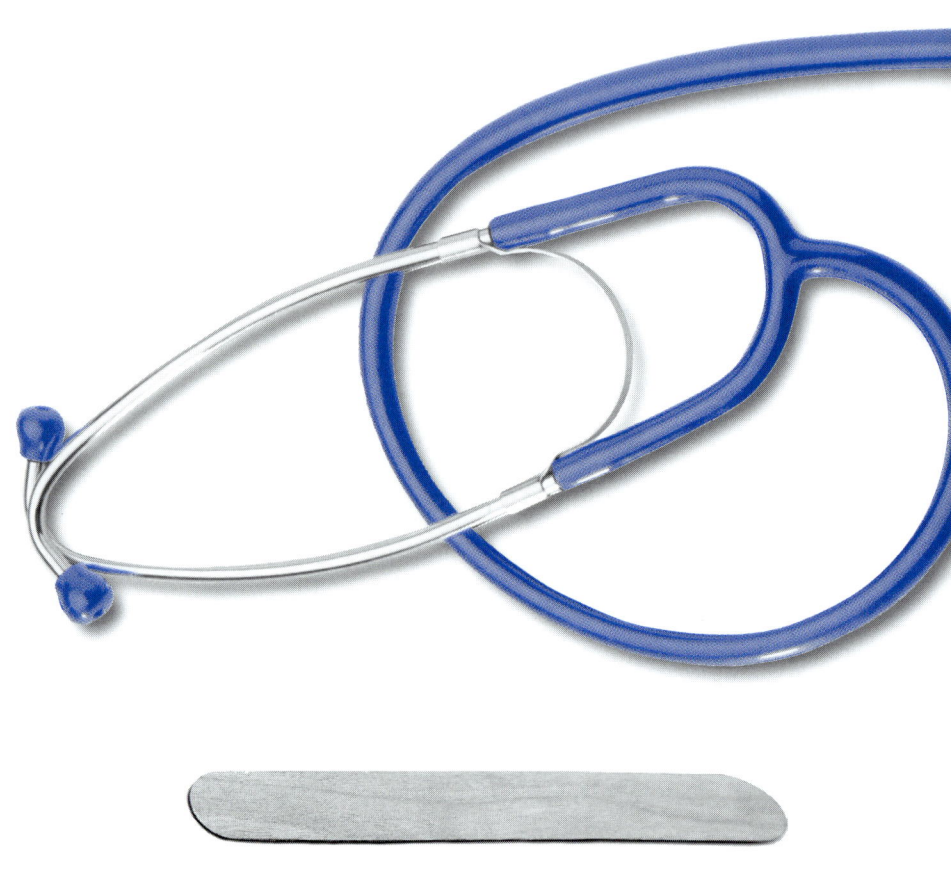

*The art of progress is to preserve order amid change
and to preserve change amid order.*

−Alfred North Whitehead

How Fit Is Your Business Model?

A business model, like any other part of an organization, will benefit from a periodic review no matter how well it seems to be working. Given these volatile economic times, we're learning the hard way: What worked well yesterday may be obsolete today. Right before our eyes we're witnessing how whole industries are changing at warp speed. Take, for example, telephone service. The home-wired phone (a.k.a. the landline) is being replaced with a mobile phone as the primary phone, and in some homes the only phone. Yes, the good old-fashioned landline is going the way of the dinosaur.

If you think that only international conglomerates are at risk, you're not seeing reality squarely. Any company, regardless of size, is up against external forces that may put them at risk. Most companies have found that the most cost-effective way to improve the health of their business model is to start with the assumption that at least an adequate business model is in place and to look for some version of the Japanese *kaizen* model of continuing improvement over time.

The concept of *kaizen* is one of restructuring and reorganizing every aspect of a system to ensure it remains at peak efficiency. The major areas where a business model can be updated or looked at critically both throughout the year and annually are the budget process and through special projects that are normally handled by a company's financial planning and analysis process (FP&A) function. The FP&A function can be located in accounting, operations, or sales depending upon the company and industry.

The Rule of Eight

First let's determine which people in your organization need to be part of this business model review process. I use the eight-person rule of thumb when it comes to solving (almost) any problem within a company. Why the magic number eight? For the simple reason that most companies (traditional and emerging) form their operations around some version of eight basic functional areas. (This does not include ancillary functions like legal, purchasing, research and development.)

The key function areas include some combination of accounting, finance, sales/marketing, operations, manufacturing, information technology, human resources, and customer service. If your company doesn't have eight functional areas, just make sure that each department is represented in the model review process. (The smallest group I facilitated was a two-person technology firm with a product vision expressed on PowerPoint slides.) The composition of the team more often than not consists of key middle-level managers, as opposed to C-level officers. Most C-level officers respect the expertise of the eight people and are comfortable with their recommendations provided that the group keeps the C-level officers well informed.

When selecting the team leader for such a project, consider the value of process expertise and leadership skills to manage the review. These are important considerations for two main reasons:

1. Often a crucial role of the group or leader is to understand when corporate-level business decisions are needed to solve the issue; and

2. When that corporate-level business decision is needed, the leader must have the ability to clearly articulate that situation and obtain the business decision(s) needed by the group.

How Fit is Your Business Model?

The Framework

Some of the best places to look to tweak an existing model for rapid short-term payback are the areas below.

1. Create an executive planning dashboard focusing on five to seven company wide key results you want to track as critical success factors for your business. Three of the more commonly used critical success factors (often called metrics) are sales backlog, new business closed, and number of employees in the company or department being examined. Resource 2 presents a version of a Flash Report where the company is extremely concerned about cash and consequently tracked key liquidity factors on the business summary financials.

   Although it sounds simple to ask what are the five to seven key issues to track and monitor, this is usually a Herculean effort. But once the key business drivers have been identified, you can work backwards to ensure those factors are key assumptions in other areas particularly the budget or planning process mentioned earlier. Also, by determining what the real business drivers are before the budgeting process, or even during the process, management knows or will learn those five to seven most crucial factors to monitor and manage, rather than getting lost in mountains of data and trying to measure everything.

2. The next step involves analytic recaps and periodic sanity checks to see that the budget meets your "sanity check" requirement. This usually includes a number of financial yardsticks involving revenues, expenses or profits relative to various industry norms, and return on equity or return on investment projections. One of the simplest sanity checks to compute is revenue per employee. This ratio can

also be one of the most valuable because most industries publish detailed versions of revenue per employee results.

If your business model or budgetary process does not create a balance sheet as part of that process, create those projected balance sheets as soon as possible. Although you'd think that I should no longer be surprised at what errors or risks show up when balance sheets are added to the process, I still get surprised. One of the most common surprises companies find looming are near-term cash shortages. This happens because until the balance sheet is added, sources of cash to accomplish the desired business goals are not considered.

One slightly different version of a sanity check relates to using at least a rule of thumb for valuations obtainable. Now I always use at least a $20-million-revenue target because of one client's surprise. Two key executives asked me to help them relaunch an incredibly successful company, which had been sold several years earlier at the top of the market. We created a business plan, presentation and projections to relaunch a portion of the business they acquired. Later, I estimated net proceeds for them after getting on track to create their $10-million-business unit. The problem was that they wanted net proceeds more than twice that amount. Working to project the business results needed to reasonably obtain those cash-out amounts suggested targeting $20 million in revenue. (In most industries $20 million in revenue is a level that buyers find more appealing. After all, there will be more infrastructure, better systems, and often a better trained workforce.) When I explained this to my client, they had a problem. They told me they could realistically target building a $10 million company, but they could not dream big enough to build a $20 million company! Resource 5 provides a basic valuation recap.

3. Finally, it is important to view the Budget and Business Plan process as a tool for ongoing business decisions and feedback. Far too many companies think of the budgeting process as the "Excel Hell" period to be completed as soon as possible, rather than taking the last 5% to 10% of time for strategic thinking and contingency planning.

Now that your company has adopted a more strategic approach to planning or budgeting, what is the next issue that can arise to slow down or prevent you from reaching your company's goals and visions? Think of this issue as a clear stream of water, which can flow through the countryside to the beautiful ocean. The ocean can be your target objective for the company. The stream is the operational process or information flow that is needed to manage the company well, and reward employees and shareholders.

When difficulties stop the stream's progress, bottlenecks, dams or blockages occur. Where there is one blockage, often additional blockages will occur. One of the most visible examples of those blockages is the company's inability to get the data to make the decisions needed to run the company strategically. Researching why that occurs often pinpoints areas upstream where other small or large blockages have built up over time. Since most companies have developed and adopted a business model and now are executing on that model through their internal budgeting process, let's talk about making what many companies call Excel Hell into something more strategic. For those of you laughing and saying my middle-market company uses SAP, Oracle, etc., and we do not have Excel Hell month or quarter, check around and listen for phrases like "island of data," "going offline," or "checking up on accounts." When you see how many Excel or even manual steps exist to support the pretty sophisticated report you receive, send me your story for the next book.

Our goal is to do away with painful Excel-based budgeting marathons and turn your budget into a strategic tool to improve the bottom line. This framework uses the budget process to help companies manage risk while reaping the rewards of achieving their corporate goals. This jingle says it all: *Inch by inch, life's a cinch. Yard by yard, life is hard.* Let's see if we can change the budgeting dynamic to make sure we eliminate the chance that *cell by cell, budgeting is hell.*

Strategic budgeting achieves the following results:

○ Easy to prepare and use

○ Easy to get buy-in with all departments

○ Easy to integrate into your corporate plan

○ Drive incentive plans to reward targeted behavior

○ Make the process next year even better

Shaping Up Your Budget

The following are my 21 favorite tips to turn Excel Hell budgeting into a strategic management tool that helps build or maintain your business model:

1. Determine the five to seven companywide key business issues.

2. Use those issues in a key business issues report logic that runs through the budget framework and philosophy.

3. Create a standard Excel input template to reduce Excel Hell.

4. Standardize charts of accounts and reporting formats.

5. Emphasize that budgets are done on a monthly basis, not as a total divided by 12.

6. Meet with departmental heads to help them see the budget as a tool, not as a weapon.

7. Build from the bottom up by department so departmental ownership is created.

8. Present results in a manner understandable to line management and department managers.

9. Involve department heads so they own the process and results.

10. Minimize the use of allocations where possible to increase user confidence in numbers.

11. Move toward some version of flexible quarterly budgeting process.

12. Use software packages that show underlying details so users can research and understand variances form budgets.

13. Use both realistic budget targets and stretch budgets to manage and integrate with your incentive plans.

14. Integrate with some version of Balanced Scorecard, which balances strategic non-financial performance measures to traditional financial metrics.

15. Provide historical 12-month income statements for users to review for the budget process and then incorporate them in their ongoing review of budget comparisons to identify trends early on.

16. Hold people accountable for their budgets.

17. Create a transition path to move to budgetary software modules that are now becoming much more reasonable in price.

18. Create key inputs on the Executive Dashboard so you can refine "what if" scenarios.

19. Create at least one scenario that is far in excess of believability on both the upside and downside.

20. Make sure your board understands the business risks the company is taking as identified in the budget.

21. Use the budget to support soft (read: non-financial) goals.

Bonus Tip: Pull this list out every six months to see how you can better manage your company's operations and resultant cash flow. Feel free to add notes or comments and change any words to "make it your own." After all, you gain when you internalize information.

 Coming Up

There's a colorful maxim about not being able to make a silk purse out of a sow's ear. But when it comes to those pesky pricing models not measuring up even though you can't afford to toss them out, the FiscalDoctor is ready to start mending. We'll take a look at the fix in Chapter 7.

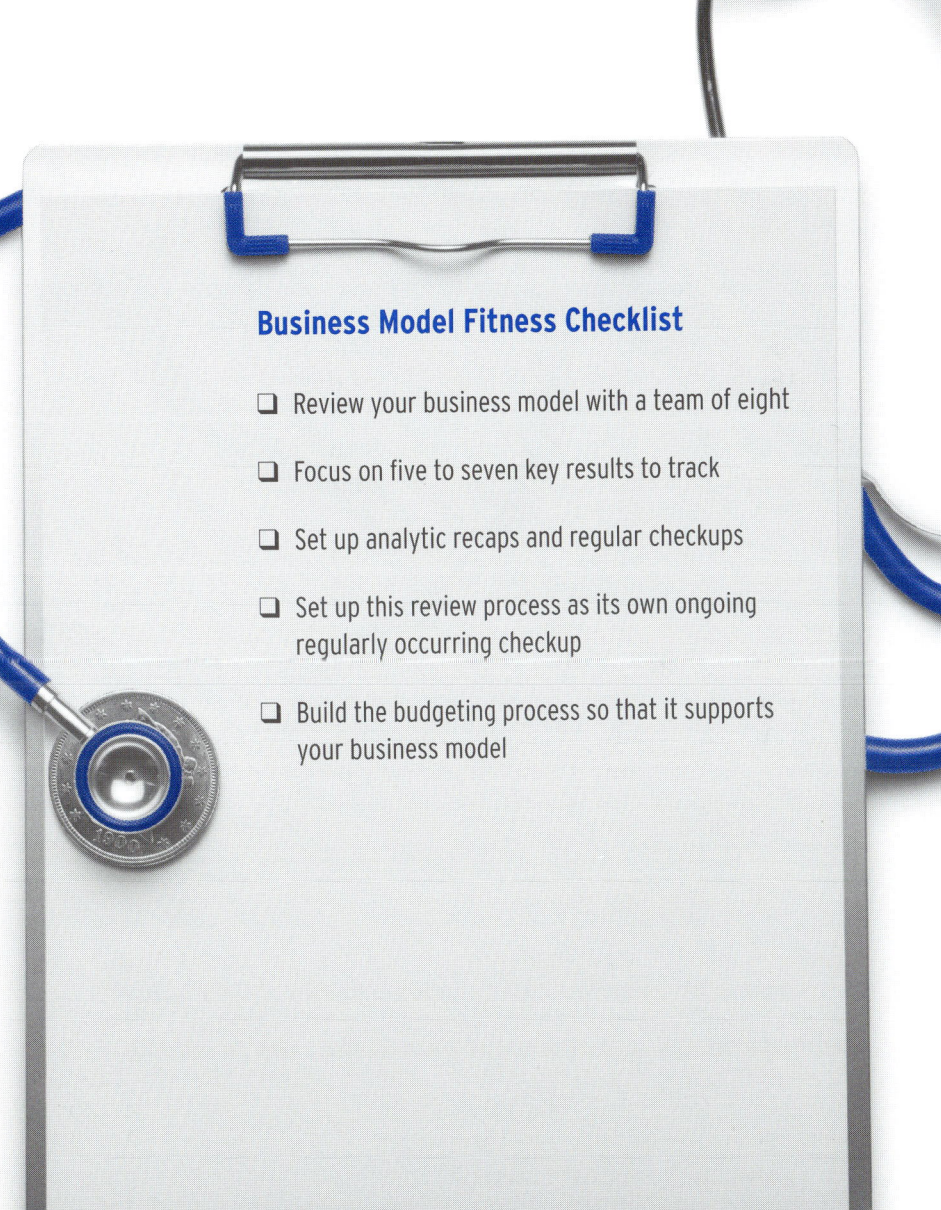

Business Model Fitness Checklist

- ❏ Review your business model with a team of eight
- ❏ Focus on five to seven key results to track
- ❏ Set up analytic recaps and regular checkups
- ❏ Set up this review process as its own ongoing regularly occurring checkup
- ❏ Build the budgeting process so that it supports your business model

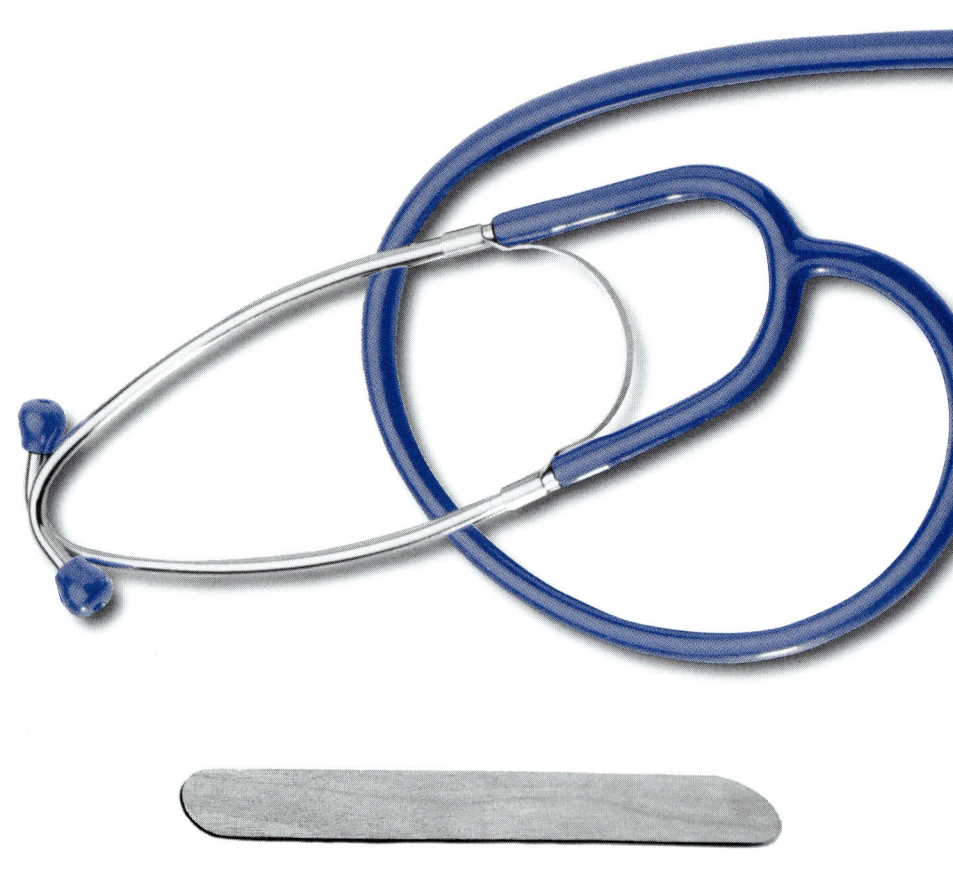

*I cannot say whether things will get better if we change;
what I can say is they must change if they are to get better.*
—Georg C. Lichtenberg

Breathe New Life Into Your Pricing Model

Is your pricing model showing its age? Or worse, is it just about to collapse, but you still desperately need it to meet this year's budget or cash constraints? The following scenarios may be an indication that your pricing model is in need of some attention:

○ Your accounting department reports that you are losing money on certain types of sales

○ Even worse, the accounting department is unsure, but "thinks" you are losing money on certain types of sales

○ Your sales department complains that it can't get needed information to make proposals in a reasonable time

○ Even worse again, your customers complain about the turnaround time of your proposals

Because it is critical to take corrective action without causing a major disruption to your customers, this chapter outlines an incremental action plan that you can immediately implement until you're in a better position to overhaul your pricing model. An incremental approach quickly begins improving your model to help increase, or at least maintain your profit margin to begin providing the funds needed for a newer model that better fits your needs and that allows you to incorporate the strategic changes you make according to the FiscalDoctor's Best Practices.

The examples in this chapter view "pricing model" as a tool used to support quotes and process given to customers to win business, where something is unique about the bid submitted. Depending on your industry, you may have a different understanding of the phrase "pricing model." Some readers may see a pricing model more as a product management tool. Regardless of how you define it, this approach will breathe new life into what you are currently using. The key requirement is to revisit the model regularly to make the pricing process or margin maintenance replicable.

This chapter breaks the suggestions into two phases. Phase One involves four immediate actions that you can take to breathe new life into your existing model. Phase Two provides the framework for obtaining your "dream" pricing model.

Phase One

1. Analyze the existing pricing model framework. Whether you glean data from the "official computer system" or from anecdotal departmental summaries, your executive team must ask fundamental questions to ensure your pricing model supports the company's key current and future business as well as operational realities. Key questions to ask are:

- Regardless of what the official system says, how do managers see the business actually running?

- Is our pricing model fully automated, or are some parts handled manually?

First, let me point out that the major reason a company encounters pricing model problems is directly related to changes in a company's product line and its competitive environment. Therefore, the older your pricing systems, the more likely you will find you are selling different types of products than in the past. Those different products may require new approaches on estimating, costing, or pricing that do not fit well with the existing pricing model.

Breathe New Life Into Your Pricing Model

For example, I once worked with a $100-million steel company briefly mentioned in a previous chapter that had invested in software and hardware systems that served it well when its business was the high volume manufacturing of a limited number of products with a limited choice of options. Over the years, the industry became much more competitive. Customers demanded and got a wider range of options. The business had to change from selling standard high-end steel building products to selling custom-engineered products. While the existing pricing model had been created to support estimates based on product standard costs (where a limited number of products were sold in large quantities), nearly every new sale now included a much broader range of products to meet new demands for a plethora of colors, lengths, width, height, and architecturally appealing glass sections. The new demands could no longer be handled by the company's old systems. This meant that EVERY sales proposal and bid required a unique pricing model. It was a perfect and typical example of why unofficial Excel spreadsheet systems often spring up in various departments. This bottleneck created an ongoing nightmare for the company's estimating department.

However, when we asked, *What systems or procedures are manual or semi-manual?* the answers we received helped us isolate the key weaknesses of the old system. We quickly came up with an effective hybrid solution that allowed us to continue using the old computer system/pricing model while customizing our major material pricing structure. How did we do this? We went offline and drew on the expertise of a qualified cost accountant who manually created new prices that covered a wider range of products, using a banding concept. The new prices were then fed into the computer system. This allowed our existing pricing model to remain functional, while we moved to a more modern system.

2. What do we sell and to whom? With the help of your sales force and marketing departments, compare and contrast your company's current customer contracts to your ideal target customer profile. Your sales team can obtain critical customer market information by reviewing sales and prospects reports, as well as purchasing industry research studies at a reasonable cost. With this new information, you're prepared to ask questions such as, *Which customers are most profitable now and will be in the future? What aspects of our products do they value most?* This thought process can often be the impetus to redefine the profile of your ideal target customer (described in more detail later as a Phase Two action) and create a marketing or business plan that targets that ideal customer profile. This plan can be as simple as modifying your sales strategy to include a mix of current clients and new prospects.

3. Reconcile "dueling spreadsheets" and silo thinking. Far too many companies have dueling spreadsheets where each department has a unique and/or a different way of interpreting and recording product costs, customer sales, and other associated profits and losses. Not only does a "silo" mentality create animosity, distrust, and biases among departments, but more important, it results in chaotic and conflicting views on your pricing structure, making communication and decision making difficult.

If you want to improve your pricing model, you need to meet with every department to understand the different factors they consider critical and identify where the numbers they have for those factors are different from the accounting department's numbers. Out of those meetings, updated information to create a more correct cost model will often emerge covering disputed issues like capacity, product cost, and customer retention prediction. A follow-up round with each department and then a combined meeting of all departments can result in a consensual understanding of your pricing model. In the end, the atmosphere will become less politically and emotionally charged, and your executive team will be in a better position to tackle the hard numbers in your pricing model based on facts, not on gut or politically fueled feelings.

4. Adjust the model to reflect the issues identified in the preceding steps. Select an internal or external facilitator to lead this process and support him or her by stressing cross-departmental participation from everyone involved in the prior steps. Make the leader responsible for prioritizing the challenges and issues that were identified and for creating two lists—an "A" list and a "B" list—that highlight the estimated costs and benefits associated with each task. As a tiebreaker on the inevitable issues that are hard to split between A and B tasks, the leader should pick those that can be completed immediately to maintain momentum. To build team spirit and a winning attitude, identify one or two "A" tasks that can be achieved easily. It's important to obtain feedback and participation from your team to finalize your roadmap, while continuing to ensure user involvement when adjusting your pricing model.

Moving Forward from This Update Base into Phase Two

Using some form of the prior actions—of course, adapting them to what works best at your company—you will improve your company's profitability and cash flow enough to begin funding a new integrated system that will enable you to meet current sales requirements. As you move into Phase Two, as outlined below, be sure you create a follow-up system on Phase One that combines periodic check-ins both by time and milestones of tasks completed. It's amazing what recognition and small celebrations of milestones will do to maintain high morale and buy-in and make the ultimate revisions envisioned in Phase Two that much easier to accomplish.

Finally, never lose sight of your objective to spotlight critical areas where pricing or costing changes will almost immediately improve your bottom line and generate more profit without dramatically overhauling the pricing model. If you keep your eye on improving your pricing model today, the day will come when you'll be able to fund your dream pricing model. As much as software prices have decreased in recent years, your dream system may not require as dramatic a champagne budget as you thought.

1. Identify your ideal customers and determine how you can sell to them. Using elements of the information developed earlier to better understand your customers, examine how their profitability impacts your ability to retain them as customers, and estimate how changes in their needs will impact your business. Think of this as diving deeper than the time-honored question of "What is our target market niche and what can I do to provide a service and/or solve a problem of my customer?"

In the modern world, perfection is seldom possible, but neither is it necessary. A number of you will say you have very little information, or are unsure of its accuracy. Don't use that as an excuse to do nothing. Recognize the range of those unknowns and start creating something on a pilot basis. As the data (and your ability to interpret it) improves, it will become more and more useable.

At a minimum, talk about these questions:

- Which customers are most profitable now and will be more profitable in the future?

- What aspects of our product do they value and why?

- What are our competitive advantages and disadvantages?

Researching these questions, and a few others that you feel are appropriate for your company, often suggests product extensions, new products, feature changes and/or improvements needed to keep existing products and services fresh and appreciated by customers. Closely examining recent contracts and the present sales funnel can be useful in creating a target customer profile.

2. What are the present system constraints and limitations? A key requirement of software or process implementations is to fully understand limitations of the old system to better specify requirements for the new system. If you don't understand your system's limitations, you may find yourself continuing to create irrelevant data — a "garbage in, garbage out" situation or a nightmare.

Hershey is a point in case. Several years ago Hershey rolled out a new software system, an SAP R/3 system, which tried to simultaneously implement enterprise resource planning (ERP), customer relationship management (CRM) and supply chain management systems. That sounds great except for the fact that the system severely damaged the company's ability to ship and sell candy over a peak holiday season. Estimates were that $150 million in sales were lost. Although all the facts never came out, the consensus was that implementation failed because of poor handling of the soft issues — communication with management and users, training and lack of testing before going live. Fortunately, the problems were resolved later and the system conversions were successfully completed. Bottom line: Be sure to better plan for all the soft issues of any new software system or conversion, including pricing models.

Once you have completed the preceding steps, key areas to analyze will become apparent. In many companies this will include reviewing in more detail multiple vendor software systems (ranging in sophistication from QuickBooks, DacEasy,

SBT, Peachtree, Solomon, Platinum, Timberline, and Great Plains, to Oracle, JD Edwards, or SAP). Don't be surprised to learn that your people are using systems from companies that no longer exist or have been acquired by a company that has no intentions of providing more than minimal upgrades or support. You may even need to analyze homegrown niche retail and internet shopping cart systems, Excel and Access applications —where data is manually entered and journal entries created for the official systems; and reviews of billing information and progress status by operational managers.

I once worked with a company that used 40-plus different database/systems in their information flow. This meant that at any one point in time, different users got different answers on an issue depending upon which of the 40 systems they were on. (Can you spell *n-i-g-h-t-m-a-r-e*?) Yet the executive team wondered why their managers complained that they didn't get needed information timely to run the business. To the Board and CEO, this data logjam was invisible. After all, there were multiple professional-looking computer generated statements to meet monthly financial statement and auditing needs, with more supporting data than any human being could digest, particularly within the short time frame given to analyze and use the data. Unfortunately, this is a far too typical case of drowning in data while not receiving the appropriate information to manage a business.

3. Identify additional business constraints the new pricing system must address. As mentioned at the start of the chapter, the need to revise or update your pricing model normally occurs because your products have changed dramatically over time. Now is the time to do a thorough job of identifying those changes—both in your overall business and your products—so your description of your "dream" pricing model is as close to perfect as possible. Going even further, I recommend you invest the extra time to anticipate some of the new features or business you will be handling in the next few years. The more flexibility you give yourself now, the longer your new pricing model will last.

Questions that are helpful in such a process include the following:

- What are the issues that delay bids, manufacturing, or require extra resources to meet customer demands?

- Why are extensive software revisions needed when we add features required for new customers?

- What new features or products do our customers want that our pricing model should be able to handle in the future?

You may also be surprised at the amount of uncertainty and disagreement among departments as to which items are variable expenses and what the true business drivers of your business actually are. Answering these questions and getting a consensus among departments is a critical early step in creating a viable, reliable pricing system.

4. Sanity check. Somewhere in your process of creating the new pricing model, be sure to run some sanity check results from the existing pricing system on the new system. (Remember the Hershey story. One of the problems identified after the fact, was the need to do have done more testing of transactions before going live on the new system.)

One of the advantages of looking at the preceding issues on a test basis is that you can analyze what does not seem to work without spending any money. When followed up properly, you should then get better results through applying and using the information you have been gathering. And finally, you must determine what changes are needed to the model so your company can run them if needed and implement a follow-up or review process.

 **Coming Up**

We mentioned earlier the need to get the data to run your business on a timely basis. In Chapter 8, I provide Best Practices and specific ways to get crucial information in your hands when you need it.

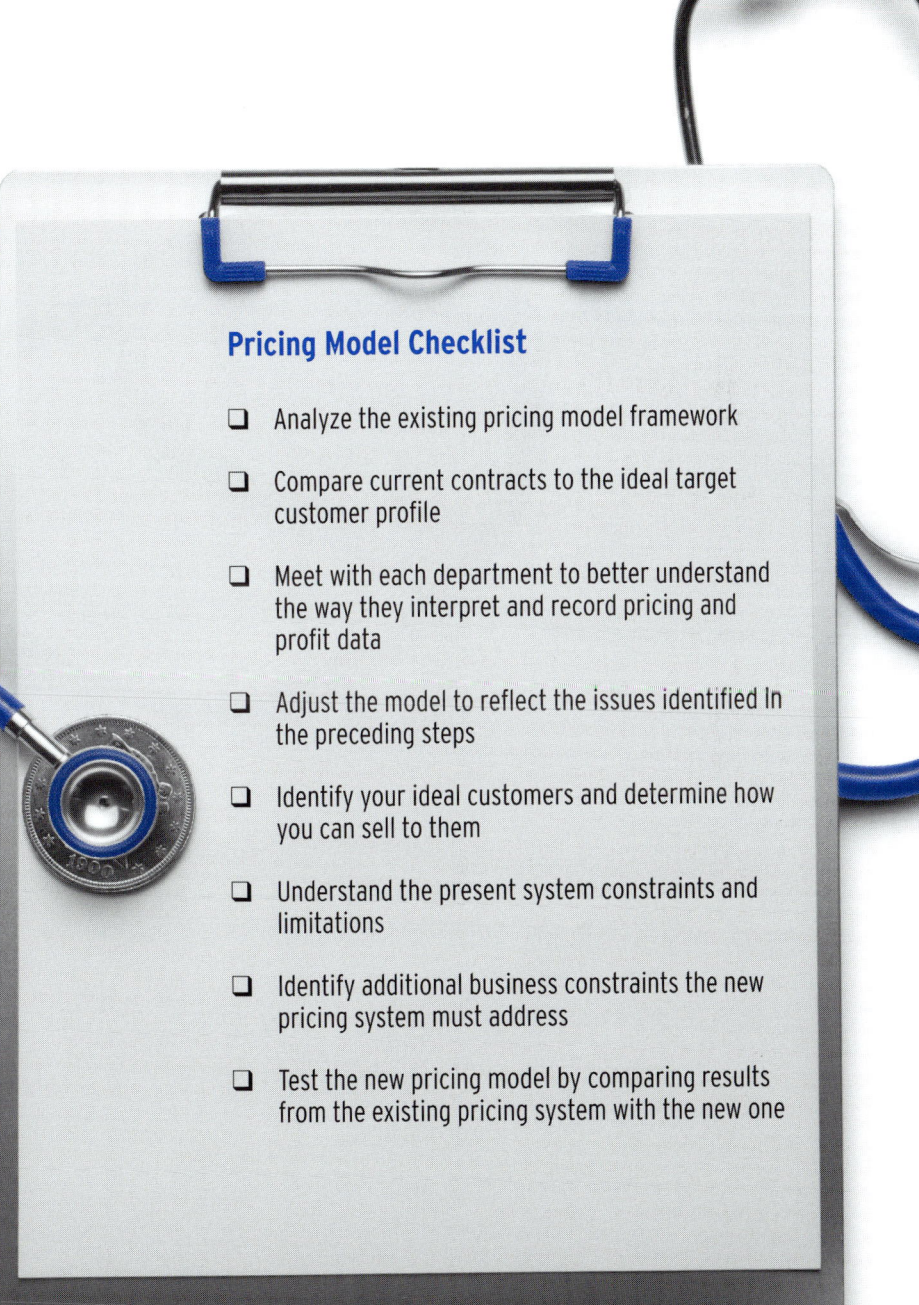

Pricing Model Checklist

- ❏ Analyze the existing pricing model framework
- ❏ Compare current contracts to the ideal target customer profile
- ❏ Meet with each department to better understand the way they interpret and record pricing and profit data
- ❏ Adjust the model to reflect the issues identified In the preceding steps
- ❏ Identify your ideal customers and determine how you can sell to them
- ❏ Understand the present system constraints and limitations
- ❏ Identify additional business constraints the new pricing system must address
- ❏ Test the new pricing model by comparing results from the existing pricing system with the new one

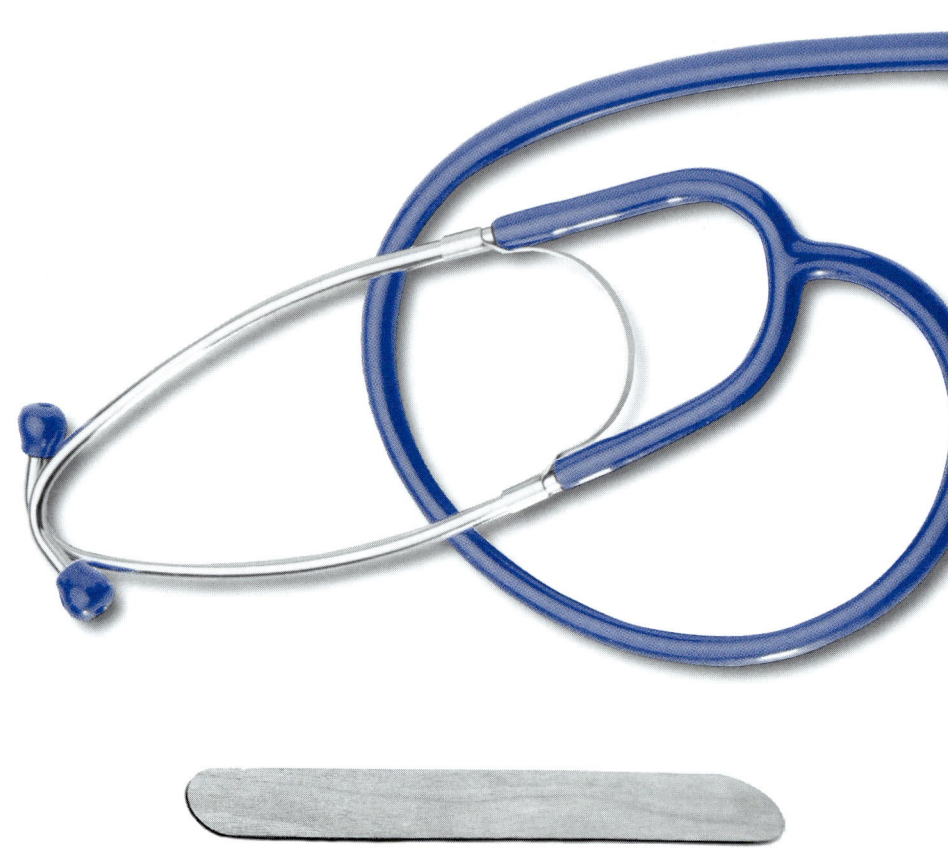

*Knowledge is a process of piling up facts;
wisdom lies in their simplification.*

–Martin Fischer

Stress Test: Show Me the Data (on Time!)

For lack of a nail, a shoe was lost. For lack of a horse, a kingdom was lost. This adage is well known, even though the source was lost long ago. The concept of taking care of the basics applies to every area all the way up to the level of corporate board of directors. It goes without saying that a CEO and his or her executive staff will be able to make informed, quality decisions in a timely fashion, time and again, if and when they consistently receive the relevant information in a timely fashion. Conversely if you're unable to get the data you need, you may find yourself making decisions in a vacuum, which is a very dangerous position for a decision maker.

I suggest the easiest way to begin an evaluation of the quality of the data available within a company and to executive management is to review the Board of Director's information package. After all, your company's board package is supposed to be the most focused strategic information available concerning your business. Anything missing or poorly assembled is a symptom of an underlying problem in the data needed to make the best business decision.

For decision makers reading this chapter who do not report to a board of directors, change the phrase board of director to your boss's title.

Why is it that top management at some companies wonder if they are getting full value from their board of directors, while board members are equally frustrated by how poorly the company's management supports them? More often than not, some or most of the answer may be as simple as not getting the right data to board members at the right time. Have you ever stopped to ask yourself why boards don't get the data they need to make timely and informed decisions? Or why so many board members view distributing a board of director's package well in advance of the meeting as a foreign concept?

If the phrase "well in advance" doesn't raise eyebrows, another sobering reality usually does — the fact that board packages are not typically finalized until one to three days before board meetings. In worst-case scenarios, some material may not be distributed until the night before with updates handed out as board members walk into the meeting. With time lines like that, you can forget about well-thought-out, considered decision making no matter how many corporate titans or geniuses sit on your board.

Informed Decisions

Ironically, these are the same companies that profess to understand the value of making informed decisions to increase profitability and sales by relying on timely reporting and delivery of key business and financial metrics, as well as information sharing, open communication, conflict resolution, and relationship-building skills among their divisions and reporting structures. While companies of all industries and sizes are guilty of this contradictory behavior, I've found this is especially true of high-growth companies.

In raising the question, "*Why don't board members get the data they need to make informed decisions?*" this chapter brings to light some of the key underlying reasons and offers practical steps and "new" insights that will improve the delivery time of documents to board members, thereby making board meetings more productive and effective.

Underlying Reasons

Timing the release of critical information is a way for executives to control their boards. There are some CEOs who think their job, ipso facto, is to manage or control their boards by deciding when and how to release controversial or sensitive information. The reasons for doing this are as varied as the personalities of the CEOs. Stories abound of executives who have ripped out offending pages of completed board packages right before the books were distributed. Fortunately, the increased level of corporate governance is discouraging this kind of behavior, but it still exists.

Inefficient or inadequate accounting processes create bottlenecks for collecting timely and critical financial data. Not all accounting departments are created equal. In fact, there are many accounting departments that simply don't have the capability to prepare, analyze, and distribute the financials well in advance of a board meeting. Typically this happens in companies that are understaffed or where software systems are unwieldy and/or not kept current.

This particular problem is especially true of companies that are in growth mode or undergoing a major change. For example, one company I worked with had an arduous process of creating and consolidating financial statements. It took more than 100 steps and six different accounting systems to create monthly financial statements. And this was the improved process! While this may be an extreme example, it's not hard to imagine how difficult it can be to get timely data when there are too many layers of information to wade through or too many processes to perform.

Information from marketing, sales, and technology departments is not easily attainable. If you think it's difficult to gather critical financial information within a given department, how difficult do you think it is for departments across a company to work together to collect, analyze, and interpret marketing, sales, and technology reports for board meetings? If you said almost impossible, you'd be right on point. I find, however, that there are many cases that amount to nothing more than excuses or sloppy practices. Some examples are:

- Our company is moving too fast to accurately collect or track such information.

- Our company is undergoing dramatic change.

- Our company is not in a financial position to tap outside resources to conduct a rigorous, much-needed marketing, sales, or technology analysis that may give us useful additional information that we can use in our board packages.

- If any of these sound familiar, send me your best stories you have heard or used for a future edition of this book.

The company doesn't have the bandwidth to adequately prepare for board meetings. The sad truth of many high-growth companies is that they just don't have the time, resources, and people power to collect the essential information for board meetings. I've witnessed companies that are so caught up in the basics of the day-to-day operations (i.e., selling services, manufacturing products, handling customer service) that management doesn't have the capability to collect and distribute good, timely information for board meetings; let alone prepare for board meetings.

Taking Steps to Rectify the Situation

If the journey of a thousand miles begins with a single step, how can companies begin to provide board members with timely, accurate, and valuable information? I suggest the following steps as an excellent starting point.

Step 1: Commit to breaking the data logjam. The most important step a CEO can take to come to terms with this problem is to make it a priority. By breaking whatever data logjam exists, more timely and accurate data will flow throughout the company and into the corporate board package sooner than it did last month. This means the CEO must take the initiative to appoint an executive to head a project on how to accelerate whatever system exists for collecting data for the board package, while maintaining or improving the quality of data being delivered.

Management should determine the time frame in which this data should be collected. The appointed executive should also be given the authority to mobilize resources to meet those goals. Obviously, this person needs to have the political clout and/or sponsorship to get cooperation of the project throughout the organization. This is critical because if the project is perceived as being either an accounting or IT exercise, it almost certainly will fail. (In case you question whether or not this step is needed for companies of your size, let me reassure you that I have done this for companies both under $100 million of revenue and in the several hundred million dollar revenue range.)

Step 2: Find out who worked on the logjam issue (or at least proposed solutions) in the past. I've often discovered that whenever management begins to examine an issue, they'll often find that a group from accounting, marketing, or technology has previously addressed this problem and provided solutions for breaking the cycle. Management usually finds that either the report produced was considered to be too functionally oriented for top management to appreciate, or that "it wasn't the right time" to address the issue. If your company is going down this path for the second time, it's important to unearth this information, review it, and talk to the "historian" who knows what happened and can give you insight into why this effort was not successful.

It's the CEOs job at this point to use this failed effort as a springboard to refine or create a new strategy. Think of it this way: If you don't understand why something failed in the past, you may go down the same path and fail again. Alternatively, your past mistakes may hold the key to future success.

Step 3: Streamline the collection, analysis, and distribution of data. As was raised earlier, critical information may be difficult to obtain and analyze in a timely manner. If this is the case in your company, management may want to consider taking corrective measures such as:

- Tightening the financial statement closing timetables

- Improving or overhauling the operating or financial reporting systems

- Eliminating some reports altogether and redirecting the resources to focus on higher value issues

Step 4: Simplify the board package and make board meetings more strategically focused. In my experience working with and on boards, I've found that often the level of information and the number of pages in board packages are more dense and bulkier than they need be. Presenting operational and financial information in both graphical and numeric formats can be overdone and unnecessary. You need only look at the glazed-over expressions of board members to understand the consequences of information overload.

I recommend that management put away lengthy PowerPoint presentations, white boards, and pointers and instead provide board members with one-page financial and operational summaries that are written at a strategic level. (Resource 2 contains an example of a one-page Flash Report.) Imagine how much more useful a meeting would be if management encouraged their boards to engage in a dialogue about strategic issues facing their companies instead of drowning them with company minutia.

Realizing the Benefits

The benefits of delivering timely information to board members cannot be overstated. The obvious and not so obvious reasons are:

- Directors who get the materials early are given the time to prepare and think about the issues at hand. Therefore they are able to offer more insightful, well-thought-out recommendations. A complementary benefit is that board members are encouraged to raise the company discussion to a strategic level, instead of getting bogged down in tactical, operational issues. It goes without saying that using a board to solve tactical problems is not the best use of a board's expertise and time. Most of you are paying those board members well for their help. It is tough to get a return for your money when you are not providing them the tools they need — timely information.

- Company executives have an opportunity to create a corporate culture that fosters open communication and sharing of information throughout the company. There is nothing more empowering than showing your employees you value their input by asking them to contribute information strategic enough to be included in board packages.

- CEOs and their executive teams receive that rare gift of time — time to ponder, understand, and collaborate on the key strategic issues they think should be brought to their boards' attention.

- Maintaining effective internal controls over financial reporting and distribution of material makes for good governance; it's that simple!

In the end, the quality of your board's decisions is equal to the quality of the information you provide them. And, the quality of that information, in part, depends on the timeliness of the information. It's up to management to decide how to use its board and determine the types of decisions they expect the board to make. But remember: The decisions a board makes are the decisions a company must live with. That's the bottom line, end of story.

A National Association of Corporate Directors (NACD) 2007 Public Company Governance Survey found on *average* that board members receive materials 6.3 days before a board meeting, with 7 days being most frequently cited by 31.4% of respondents.

The NACD 2008 Public Company Governance Survey reported: The number of board members receiving meeting materials in hard copy has steadily declined over the past three years. In 2008, 87.5% of respondents reported receiving hard copy meeting materials, down from 93.8% in 2007 and 97.4% in 2006.

Correspondingly, receipt of electronic meeting materials (via e-mail or via Internet download) has increased to 91.6% in 2008. Directors receive electronic materials in a variety of formats:

- About two-thirds (66.7%) receive meeting materials as e-mailed attachments.
    o Most (53.4%) receive attachments that can be read by any recipient.

- A small number (13.5%) of security conscious boards encrypt files containing meeting materials before they are e-mailed.

○ 24.7% of directors download meeting materials from a website.

- Most often (15.4% of the time) this website is a part of a company operated intranet or extranet.

- In some cases (9.4% of the time) this website is part of a commercially operated board portal or other site.

(See Resource 6 "Timing Is Everything" for the FiscalDoctor's suggestion on board packages for non-public companies.)

Again for decision makers below board of director level, substitute board for your boss, and exercise your role as a manager.

 **Coming Up**

In Chapter 9, I will show you how to help keep more money in your pocket by helping you avoid some of the pitfalls companies face when they lack a contingency plan.

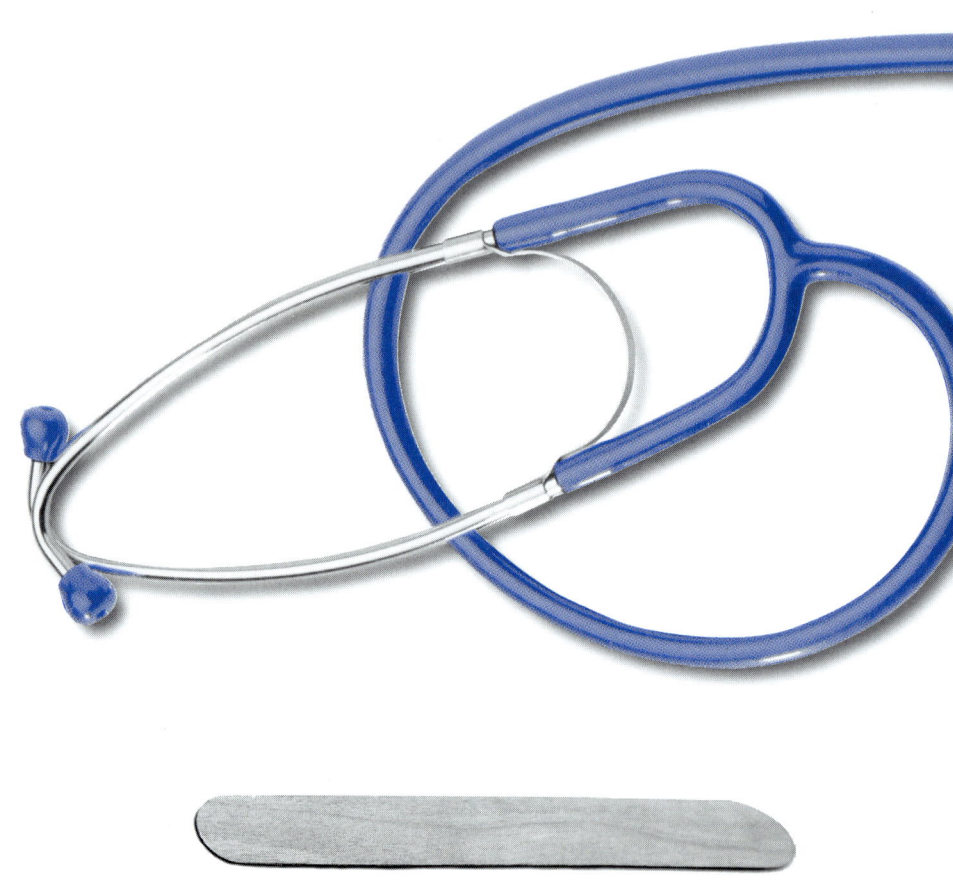

The most successful people are those who are good at plan B.

−James Yorke

ER: When Bad Things Happen to Good Companies

What would you have said two years ago if someone told you it was prudent to plan for a 20% or even 30% drop in sales from the prior year, or that internationally recognized brands like Waterford would declare bankruptcy? Does a phrase like Dr. Doom come to mind?

Think of this chapter like a meeting with your personal financial planner who wants to help you create a framework for wise investment and financial decisions. I've created a practical framework to improve your ability to deal with surprises ranging from pleasant to disasters. Yes, some companies find ways to increase sales, improve the bottom line, improve infrastructure, or even accelerate cash flow with this process. Then they can improve both internal communications to employees and external communications to the public, stakeholders, and financing sources. Other companies worry that their people have a tendency to hope problems will go away so they do not have to inform others.

Some of you will say that looking at enterprise levels of risk sounds a lot like contingency planning, an operational review, acquisition review, or even a well-laid-out budgeting or three-to-five-year business planning session. And I agree. A lot of those types of activities are the bedrock for the new enterprise risk analysis or management, also called ERM. Therefore setting up or improving some version of those stand-bys is a reasonable place to get started so that "bad things DO NOT happen to your company."

This chapter describes two phases of actions to improve your application of risk management. Phase One starts with an update on contingency planning that you can adapt or implement, and then build on that format with specific tools that can move you closer to an effective enterprise risk management process. Phase Two describes how to build on and improve the Phase One base.

What Is a Contingency Plan?

A contingency plan describes specific strategies and actions to be taken in relation to assumptions (and variances of these assumptions) that can result in a particular problem, emergency, or crisis.

- The plan should include a monitoring process and "triggers" for initiating planned actions.

- The plan should also include ways to gain stakeholder support and understanding.

- Stakeholders need to be kept informed of the reasons for any changes, the vision of the desired end result, and the proposed plan for getting there.

- The level of stakeholders' importance and influence should be considered when determining the amount of time required to gain acceptance of the plan, the timescales for implementation and completion, and the overall effectiveness of the plan.

- If time permits, input and consultation from the most influential stakeholders should be incorporated into the building of any contingency plan because without their acceptance any plan will, at best, encounter limited success.

This is where many executive teams get hung up: They know they should have a risk management program (just in case), but their management teams don't know where or how to get started. I say: In today's litigious society where plaintiff attorneys have honed the art of second guessing after the fact, do you really want to take the corporate and PERSONAL risk of not starting a risk management program? After all, extensive publicity on the need for risk management has been discussed for several years. At least set that contingency plan in motion.

Step One: Bite the bullet and get started. If you're like most companies, identifying potential risks is probably the hardest part of developing a risk management scenario. In fact, this is cited as a main reason why most companies put it off. If your management team is at a loss as to how to get started, you're in luck. Standard & Poor (S&P) has created a list of four major risk categories that can be just the springboard you need to hold your first brainstorming session. Listed in alphabetically order with supporting issues, they are:

Environmental Risks:
- Business continuity
- Business market environment
- Environmental
- Liability lawsuits
- Natural disaster/ weather
- Pandemic
- Physical damage
- Political risk
- Regulatory/ legislative
- Terrorism

Financial Risks:
- Capital availability
- Credit counterparty
- Financial market risk
- Inflation
- Interest rates
- Liquidity

Management Risks:
- Corporate governance
- Data security
- Employee health and safety
- Intellectual property
- Labor disputes
- Labor skills shortage
- M&A/restructuring
- Managing complexity
- Outsourcing problems
- Project management
- Reputation

Supply Risks:
- Commodity prices
- Supply chain

Step Two: After your team has reviewed the list, it's now time to check off the risks that apply, even tangentially, to your company.

Step Three: Review the S&P list again to see which of the risks may be catastrophic and damaging to your company. These risks warrant further consideration even if the likelihood of their occurring is very low.

Step Four: Using consensus, identify three of the most critical risks your company faces.

Step Five: Create an action plan that deals with the critical risks you've identified. The action plan should include next steps and target dates as well as those actions that may be required in the mid- and long-term future.

Step Six: Follow up on the action plan that you just created. Make sure it's executed properly.

Step Seven: Evaluate whether your next step is to dig deeper into the action plan you've created, or to move to the Phase Two suggestions below. Alternatively, if you need to consider a full-blown risk management system, move forward knowing you have benefited from the initial work. But begin as soon as possible!

Phase Two

Now that we have a foundation in place with our application of a contingency planning format base, how do we build on that in a Phase Two? Not all risks can be avoided successfully, so the focus should also be on minimizing frequency and impact and perhaps finding opportunities in risks, not just avoiding them. Which of the following suggestions might apply to your situation?

Five Targeted Questions to Move Forward

Consider the five questions below as tools to help you move further toward basic enterprise risk management. Answering the questions and improving on any of these points will accelerate your effectiveness in this area.

1. Where are we now?
2. How could we expand the three risks selected earlier to the top five to ten risks we might have now?
3. Who or what would solve or prevent the issue from happening?
4. How would we address those possibilities?
5. What would we learn from proactively doing this process?

Where is our company in terms of appreciating known risks? Some companies do an excellent job making financial and operating information available throughout their organization, conducting regular sessions with department heads, and even town hall meetings. Others limit access to information or distribution of financial statements a little more than I feel is warranted. My favorite example of the decision maker unrealistically limiting access to financial and operating information involves the owner who shared no information below the C-level yet wanted everyone to do a better job of running a high-growth company while not making mistakes. Department heads felt they received almost nothing they needed to do their business and just did the best they could in the circumstances.

Across all functional areas, I believe plans are of limited use until they are communicated clearly and effectively. Until that is done, how can top management know that the strategies and supporting tactics can be interpreted and executed correctly by people throughout the organization?

What are the top five to ten risks that are not on financial statements? Now that our team better understands the most visible potential risks, we can start to move into enterprise risk management. To understand the issues at stake for enterprise risk management, think about the Duke Lacrosse team purported sexual harassment scandal. Companies of all sizes have provided ERM examples of sexual harassment failures. All of the sexual harassment training does not seem to preclude an explosive sexual harassment incident from occurring, nor does it preclude one of your managers mishandling it. Sexual harassment, however, is just one of many risks that can blow up and damage your company's reputation if you have no plan in place.

When I help companies create a risk profile or risk road map to start or move further toward effective risk management, I start by asking the five questions below.

○ What are the three best opportunities you could create longer term and what do you need to do to best pursue those opportunities?

○ What are the top three concerns you have about meeting this year's budget?

○ What actions can we take to minimize the risk of those concerns on this year's budget?

○ What are the three top longer-term risk area concerns you have identified today and how will your management react if those concerns actually occurred?

○ What are the three most crucial infrastructure issues you face over the next one or two years? By infrastructure, I include people skills, systems and facilities.

My suggestion to limit the recap to the top five or ten items is sheer manageability. You do not need another pretty bound internal or external prepared document to gather dust. Also with tighter focus, it will be easier to evaluate how well your ERM implementation is proceeding.

Media Policy

When almost any of the examples mentioned earlier in this chapter occurs, you will be dealing with the media. With today's warp speed breaking news developments, you need to be prepared for that nightmare article in your hometown paper, or even in *Forbes* magazine. Some managers and companies are well prepared to discuss the company's position on an issue and/ or have working relationships with external communication experts. Others are either less sophisticated or hope they never have that need. You should consider identifying a resource that specializes in crisis management before you need it.

What would we learn from proactively improving our risk management process? Just the thought process of planning makes a company more flexible when something unexpected occurs. This is how successful executives maintain and even increase the lead they have over their competitors. A few companies prefer this process be outsourced with a tie to their law firm so that potentially embarrassing items that show up on the first time review are attorney client privileged information.

What Keeps Companies From Starting the ERM Process?

The 11% of you whose companies already have built ERM into your organizations can feel good or conduct a more extensive process to maintain or even increase the lead you have over your competitors. For the other 89%, you have to ask yourself, why did we drop the ball?

You may say that your team has talked about some of these issues the last time you were at a retreat or a brainstorming session. Or, you may say that senior executives and their key people are even busier than in the past, and hence inclined to see what items can be dropped, rather than accept increased responsibility to ensure future success.

Or, you may be hesitant to tackle situations where you only see the political downside to addressing an issue, "before its time." Or, it may even be the hesitancy to bring in an external resource that may uncover a concept, strategy, or missing link the executive team does not have the perspective to realize in a timely manner. Since you know your company best, you probably can add to the list. More than one speaker at some recent conferences suggested good, even strong companies, intellectually know they should follow this path and yet fail to do it.

The Bottom Line

Risk management takes time but think of the alternative. You don't want to be in a position of "would've, could've, should've" —if only we knew. When the economic climate changes as dramatically and as frequently as it does today, enterprise risk management should be on every executive's dashboard. The truth is ERM requirements are becoming mainstream and will soon be part of your corporate credit rating, and will be applied with hindsight if a risk materializes at your company by lenders, investors and trial attorneys. Ignorance is no excuse because the literature has been widely available for several years. And, because you can be held responsible for major losses that occurred under your management, sooner or later that attitude will take lots of money out of your pocket. Face your risks squarely and come up with a flexible ERM plan. Don't wait until you're forced to make a "mayday" call to a world embroiled in its own crisis.

Gary W. Patterson, The FiscalDoctor

Coming Up

Green may be the color of money, but it's also the color of the world market's changing social views. How will your company adapt to a greener marketplace, both positively or negatively?

Company Emergency Checklist

- ❏ Commit to contingency planning
- ❏ Identify risks
- ❏ Highlight catastrophic and critical risks
- ❏ Develop an action plan
- ❏ Decide whether or not to continue implementing full enterprise risk management phase
- ❏ Establish level of risk understanding
- ❏ Identify the top five to ten risks that are not included in your financial statements
- ❏ Establish media policy

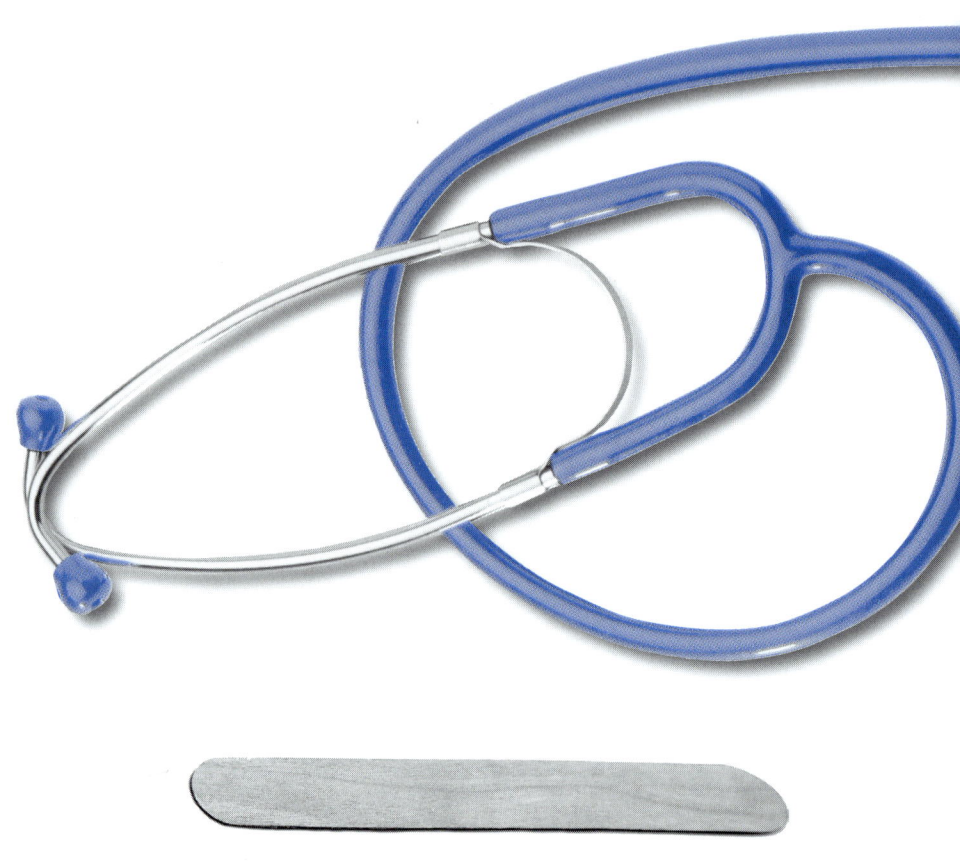

*The least movement is of importance to all nature.
The entire ocean is affected by a pebble.*

–Blaise Pascal

10

The Price of Going Green: The Good and Not So Good

There is no doubt that going green holds a certain appeal for many people. A walk down the street in any metropolitan area will yield an abundance of evidence of the green movement taking root with signs boasting everything from ozone friendly dry-cleaning and items built from partially recycled materials, to organic or locally grown food. But when it comes to business, the question isn't just about what earth friendly products your company might consider producing, it's also about being prepared for the fallout of a clean energy world.

How severely will the return to $5 or $6-a-gallon gasoline—yes the short-term blips will end sooner than you think, reflecting European gasoline prices that have been around for years—and carbon taxes (which is really what a cap-and-trade system is) on your operations or possibly those of your entire supply chain, or your power supplier being mandated to provide a geometric increase in the percentage of renewable power affect your company's operating costs and/or bottom line?

After attending several conferences on renewable energy and finance, I gleaned seven critical areas that may directly or indirectly affect an old economy industry in its attempt to compete in a clean energy world. Although renewable energy advocates admit that it's too early to predict how renewable energy will play out in the global economy over the next decade, they assert that the industries that are most prepared to meet the energy challenge will benefit the most. To paraphrase a famous quote from Benjamin Disraeli, *The secret of success is to be ready for opportunity when it comes*. In this regard, the following seven areas of concern are intended to get senior management thinking strategically about the issues of renewable energy and how best to prepare for the opportunities and challenges associated with them.

Ethanol

The energy and agriculture industries are undergoing transformational changes of historical magnitude in their efforts to produce alternative non-fossil fuel sources. The effects are already being felt with the impact increased ethanol production is having on many businesses: The term *food fight* may have new meaning as the combined impact of dramatically increased corn costs and restricted availability unfold. For those who haven't been to the movies lately, the cost of popcorn has risen 40% since 2006. The skyrocketing cost of milk is another example of how ethanol use is affecting consumer products.

Of course, the wild card is how much more are consumers willing to pay for your green products or services, either directly in taxes or indirectly in hidden costs? Another way of asking the question is, *How much of a positive or negative impact will the new green consumer attitude have on my business?*

Opportunities and Challenges

Clean energy initiatives are moving at a faster clip than originally expected: Renewable energy advocates predict that within five years such initiatives will make economic sense on a non-subsidized basis. While this prediction may be optimistic, it's a fact that larger-scale manufacturing will be affected when they are left to deal with clean energy without the benefit of receiving government subsidies either in the form of a tax credit or a grant. Thus, how businesses currently use this subsidized window of opportunity will affect their competitive position tomorrow when clean energy becomes de rigueur. In the face of present and projected government subsidies, you need to ask how your company plans to leverage federal and state tax benefits. *In other words, are you taking advantage of this grace period to build green energy facilities and processes?*

Financing Needs

A huge amount of financing will be required for targeted and foreseeable clean energy projects both domestically and globally. Estimates are in the TRILLIONS of dollars. (A trillion dollars is $1,000,000,000,000, or a million million dollars). The magnitude of those projected financing opportunities is creating a demand that many businesses have not foreseen in their recent updates of financial rates. Some may remember the 1970s when regulatory changes combined with increased demand for financing created that crowding out effect: 18% home mortgage rates and 21% short-term interest rates for businesses were the norm.

Looking back, you can see how it took less than a year for interest rates to rise to those levels. Fast forward to the present day and witness how funding clean energy projects seems to be getting more attractive and easier to do than retrofitting older facilities and start reading about the multi-TRILLION dollar estimates.

Some people say we will not see conventional energy-related products as high as in early 2008 again. After all, the world has gone from being awash with liquidity to governments pumping out money to restore liquidity and credit. Remember that major regulatory changes, which congressional leaders intend to enact, often create unintended consequences and long-term uncertainties. This is exactly what is happening to the agricultural sector where capital investment requirements are encouraging a growth in bigger corporate ownership rather than the traditional individual or family operations.

The world will return to making loans again. When that happens, you need to be ready to consider that scenario. You will need to ask how a change in funding availability and higher interest rates will affect your business. For example, how would a 1% coupon rate increase impact your business? And if you are really brave, strategize increasing that to a 2% or 3% coupon rate increase.

Clean Energy Customers

Rail and barge companies have traditionally provided transportation capacity for bulk commodities ranging from coal to grain. Today as the demand for corn and grain shipments increases, bulk shippers (and to a lesser degree trucks) are seeing their client profile change from traditional manufacturers (read: dirty energy clients) to clean energy clients. It won't be long before we see the two types of clients jockeying for transportation rights. Transportation capital investment plans are already being affected by requests for new or upgraded facilities to service clean energy plants.

For many businesses, shipment costs are buried inside other costs, so these costs may not yet be visible at the senior executive level. Thus, as a senior executive, you need to ask your purchasing and transportation departments to look into what is happening or is likely to happen to your shipping costs in the near future. In this regard, *how would either increased shipping costs or longer delivery time frames affect your business vis-à-vis the competition?*

A Carbon-Effect Economy

The likelihood of a carbon credit (read: carbon tax) is increasing worldwide and among industry giants now acknowledge it is probably inevitable. Although the United States is not a signatory, many individual states are already supporting voluntary initiatives or at least renewable electricity standards.

You may be surprised to see targeted initiatives for your state on the National Renewable Energy Laboratory website (www.nrel.gov). In addition, industry-leading companies such as Bank of America, Toyota, and Wal-Mart have green energy positions and initiatives under way, which congressional leadership does not want to end. For example, Wal-Mart plans to install solar panels to provide as much as 30% of the power for its 22 stores in California and Hawaii.

As more companies are forced to follow in the footsteps of industry leaders, *how will your company absorb the higher costs of new energy compliance requirements or taxes?*

Rising Electricity Costs

According to the U.S. Energy Information Agency, homes and commercial buildings currently use 71% of the electricity in the United States. This number is expected to rise to 75% by 2025. Rising usage is already affecting some industries, as well as consumers. For example, commercial builders are beginning to consider the benefits of installing solar rooftops. Furthermore, one of the fallouts of rising electricity costs may be reduced square footage of the average size of new residential construction.

Consumers too are taking proactive steps to control and even reduce their household electric bills by buying energy-efficient products (e.g., refrigerators, dishwashers, washers and dryers) and opting for fluorescent light bulbs over incandescent bulbs.

On the opportunity side of this issue: *Will your company be in a position to manufacture and sell new and improved products that are more energy efficient? Also, what can your company do in the foreseeable future to reduce electricity consumption of your commercial facilities?*

Water Resources

Ethanol and biomass plants require substantial amounts of water on a consistent operating basis. While this may come as a surprise to some, there is the issue of disposing of byproducts and waste from clean energy production, which involves high levels of water usage. Even before these new demands on water availability are realized, there have been spirited debates concerning who gets water and at what price. With plants being built in more areas outside of the Midwest, the issue of water allocation, availability, and price will escalate. Ask yourself: *How would higher water rates, or even allocated water consumption, affect your business or your competitors?*

While it's too early to predict exactly which moving parts of the traditional and new energy industries will interconnect to create a new energy order, one thing is clear: Executives need to use this lead time to encourage their management teams to take at least one action to either (a) tap or exploit new opportunities or (b) solve what previously may have been a nonexistent or invisible problem. Of course, your evaluation of where you stand on these clean energy issues depends upon the strength of your core business. If you're ready to take the next step, write down at least one opportunity or change needed. Trust your initial intuition and take action.

How Clean Are You?

Before going any further with this discussion, some of you may want to take a more extensive quiz on which aspects of green energy conversion you should emphasize in your strategic plan. Resource 7 contains a quiz for follow-on tactical-level planning for green energy at your company. Resource 8 contains the FiscalDoctor's suggestion for a national green policy.

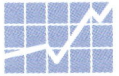 ## Coming Up

From a strong financial vision and mission to knowing your top ten customers and going green, we've nearly covered it all. But there's one more key area to cover before the FiscalDoctor gives your business a clean bill of fiscal health. In Chapter 11, we'll tie everything together and propose some ways to avoid business embarrassments.

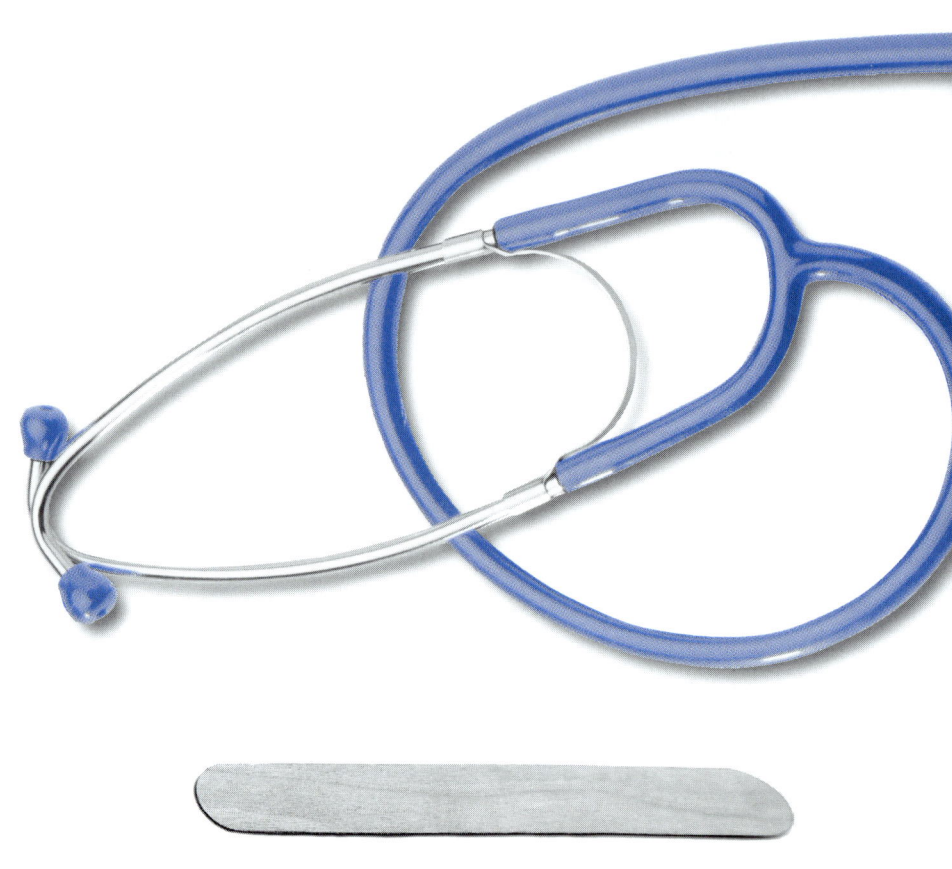

*The problem with communication
... is the illusion that it has been accomplished.*

–George Bernard Shaw

11

How Fiscally Fit Does Your Board of Directors Think You Are?

In large part, this chapter is written for your board members. Just as the President of the United States leverages the expertise of his cabinet to ensure he is making the most informed decisions for the country, CEOs (or top decision makers) tap the expertise of their outside advisers (a.k.a. board of directors) to help him/her better manage the company. The book opened with an invitation to take the FiscalDoctor's test. It seems only appropriate to come full circle and ask your company's advisers to take the FiscalDoctor's test.

Before you present the test to board members, I'd like to raise a question that was raised by none other than Jack and Suzy Welch in their *Business Week* column, "The Boardroom Bunker" (December, 25 2006-January 1, 2007). "Too often," they observed, "the question is: 'Has anything happened lately that could embarrass us?' " The sad truth is that too many boards would be forced to answer a resounding "yes." Although progress has been made to guard against governance scandals, too many board members today are in the dark—sometimes even completely clueless—when it comes to knowing the fundamental facts (read: financial health and profile) of the companies on whose boards they sit.

According to the Welchs, real progress in boardroom behavior will be evident when members can resume their rightful roles of helping to develop a strategic vision that furthers the company's growth and profitability, instead of hunkering down and peering into an abyss of financial reports. While this is a noble "meta" role, my first-hand experience with some board members tells me we're not there yet. I'm continuously amazed by what board members don't know that will indeed embarrass them if pressed against the wall. My perspective is a twist on the adage, but I believe *if you can't see the trees for the forest, you're overlooking fundamental, if not critical, knowledge of your company's business*. While the questions below may sound rudimentary— if not rhetorical—depending on your answers, you may be a deer in headlights just waiting for impact, or at least blushing with embarrassment over poor boardroom performance. You be the judge.

What is your gut reaction to where the company stands? Another way of asking this question is, "How well do you sleep at night given what you know (or don't know) about the company?" For example, based on the board package and other company materials you receive before board meetings, do things feel right, or do you have a gnawing feeling you can't quite put your finger on? After all, the board and the CEOs' credibility are impacted positively or negatively by finance, operations, sales, human resource, or communication issues. One way of gauging the reputation of the company is by checking how aggressively prestigious service providers and financial institutions seek the company's business.

Do you really know the direction in which the company is headed? If you were to begin signing Sarbanes-Oxley equivalent certifications with personal liability on current financial statements or fiscal projections, what else would you ask or want to know about the company's growth and viability? It is vitally important that boards understand the short- and long-term issues facing a company, which can be ascertained from a company's five-year strategic plan. While some may question the relevance of a five-year plan given the speed at which companies change today, I'm a proponent of long-term planning and visioning. Not only does a strategic plan act as a beacon guiding your company into the future, but just as important, it helps the board evaluate the quality of the executive team. A discussion on strategy is the surest, if not the fastest, way to learn how effective management is doing in its efforts to pull together and grow the company as a team. You'll be able to see whether management's vision is unified or splintered, which can make the difference between a company going somewhere and one that's going nowhere.

Are you receiving the communication package in a timely manner? Another concern is the timely delivery of materials prior to board meetings. If you're consistently handed materials the night before or even when the meeting starts, it's important that you note the distinction of your role in the meeting – you're viewing a presentation and not participating in a thoughtful, well-prepared business discussion. To this point, many CEOs can be great salespeople who may seduce you with their charm, wit, and fancy presentations unintentionally (I trust), thereby distracting you from observing what's really going on in the company. When was the last time you complimented the CEO on his or her effectiveness in running a board meeting and the delivery and discussion of critical strategic information? It's not a good sign if you can't remember.

What is the quality of the communication material you receive? The quality of the material will also give you a glimpse into how much you know and don't know about the company. Ask yourself if the financial reports and summaries are easy to understand and evaluate. For example, many companies drown their directors with more information than is necessary or provide too little and/or omit information on crucial areas of the company. Keep in mind the purpose of the package is to maximize the time and value of directors who have limited time to give their perspective on important issues facing the company. If you're struggling to make sense of the material—whether it's financial figures or summaries of operational issues—then you may be driven to distraction to a point where you're confounded about the health and well-being of the company.

Are the financial figures and operational metrics accurate? The timely delivery of information is critical but it's not enough. You need the assurance that past budgets, cash flow projections, sales funnel reports, and oral operational updates from the CEO and management were accurate and met. Here, the executive team's behavior speaks volumes. Ask yourself: How good are the CEO and executive team members in giving the board periodic updates on how well their past projections or assurances have been met, exceeded, or missed? If you're observing negative behavior and conflicting attitudes among the executive team in board meetings concerning the interpretation of the reports, then something may be rotten in Denmark.

Do you know who your most profitable customers are? If you can name the company's top ten customers both in terms of combined revenue and total profitability, then you're in a good position. But that's not all you need to know. You need to know the profitability of each product line as well as ascertaining how well the company meets customer requirements and response times. Again, if you're not receiving timely and accurate sales reports detailing likely customer closes, potential business, and future prospects, this may be a sign that you don't really know your profitable customers as well as you should.

Is your expertise being utilized to its fullest? Good board selection and periodic evaluations of board members ensure expert external perspectives on areas key to company growth where that expertise may not exist in the company. The value of outside expertise to a company is a major reason directors are selected by truly good or great companies. How often over the last year have you been involved in somewhat minor items like the color of an advertising brochure or details of a general ledger account such as miscellaneous expense? I trust most of you are chuckling here and hope only a few have to admit some version of this.

Where Do You Stand?

Depending on how you answered each of these questions, you can begin to measure how you feel about the health of the company you're governing.

○ I have nothing to be embarrassed about: I sleep well at night.

○ I'm mildly embarrassed: I'm above average.

○ I'm terribly embarrassed: I need to improve my performance.

○ The situation is critical: I must take immediate action.

If you're ready to take the next step, I urge you to write down three opportunities or changes needed. Resource 11 on pages 154 to 159 is set up in a format to expand those three thoughts into initial action plans. Trust your intuition. Believe me, three is enough. You can always take this quiz again to see if you've improved.

Get an Outsider's View of Your Company

Since most of the points just covered are internally focused, you should choose at least one area where outsiders react to their perception of your company. Since liquidity and financing can be the lifeblood of your company, you should find out how the company banker views the financial package they see. More often than you may want to admit, your banker and their supporting analysts are not pleased with the accuracy, visual presentation, or timeliness of company information. Accuracy may include changes to prior statements or catch-up adjustments in the current month or numbers that with minimal analytical review raise questions, if not accompanied by some brief narrative. A sloppy visual presentation may include typographical errors or poorly organized material. Timeliness ranges from being a few days to months behind.

To this point, when times are good and meeting payment terms and covenant compliance is easy, your banker may tend to overlook the company's less-than-impressive presentation. Their comments may be as gentle as asking when things will be caught up and what plan will be set in place to get things in line. At this stage, you may experience a slight twinge of embarrassment. As time continues to pass, however, that understanding may begin to erode. If and when your company ship encounters rough seas, will you be able to look the company's banker in the eye?

From determining a financial vision and mission to breaking the data logjam and better understanding your customers as well as building long-term wealth and evaluating the power of going green, you should now understand many of the habits needed to maintain your fiscal health. But like any good health and wellness program, it's not enough to acknowledge your company's issues; you must formulate the plan and be willing to carrying it out. So, after grading yourself, you need to ask one more question: *What will it take for your company to become fiscally fit?*

Doctor's Note

My sincere hope is that this book will serve as a handy resource tool that will help you burrow inside your company and examine your inner workings. Management guru Peter Drucker put it this way, *What gets measured gets managed.* As the FiscalDoctor, I like to say, *What gets examined gets attention.*

On that note, I wish your company good health, and I wish you a good night's sleep.

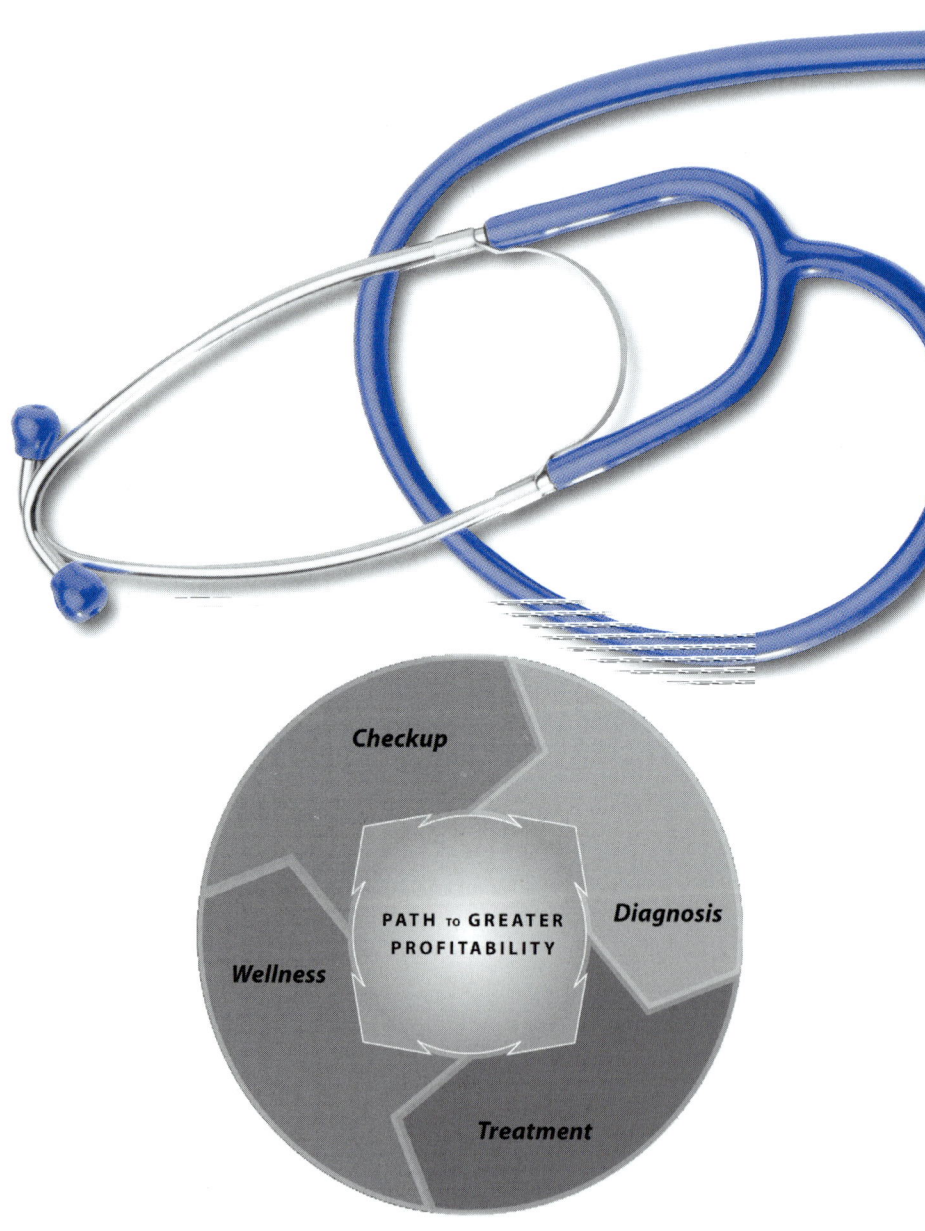

ATTAINING VISION WHILE MANAGING RISK

Resources: The Doctor's Bag

R1	Decision Making in a Vacuum	130
R2	Flash Report	131
R3	More Quantitative Approach to Risk Tolerance	134
R4	Levels of Accounting Resources	136
R5	Valuation	141
R6	Timing is Everything	143
R7	Follow-On Tactical-Level Planning for Green Energy at Your Company	144
R8	The FiscalDoctor's Recommendation for the National Green Policy	149
R9	Definitions	150
R10	Personal Notes	151
R11	First, Second and Third Actions to Take	154
R12	Do You Have a Question?	160

R1 Decision Making in a Vacuum

Additional tips for Chapter 3

Some decision makers are non-financial leaders who work with a CFO or an accounting department to implement or improve a contingency planning or ERM function in their companies. You will be pleased to know that a substantial amount of financial information is available to support your decision-making process. Below is a list of items that you should become familiar with before you engage your CFO in a discussion.

1. Balance sheets

2. Income statements

3. Budget projections (either for the rest of the fiscal year and in some cases multiple years)

4. Other supporting data of cash flow projections

5. Risk management processes

6. Prior consultant reports

 R2 Flash Report

Supporting information for Chapters 2, 6 and 8

Benefits of a Flash Report and where to use it have been discussed in several chapters. Some of you may have heard the tool used in different ways. My recommended format below is a combination of determining and monitoring a limited number of key operating items and a summarized financial snapshot provided more timely than the monthly financial statements.

The phrase "Flash Report" is used most often when the report is prepared quickly before full financial data is available. Others use a Flash Report to monitor and track the top five to seven operating items or metrics that decision makers feel are key to managing their business. The restaurant company I was part of accumulated data for a daily Flash Report that tracked sales, labor hours, food waste, and cash collected. With that information, they knew how the financials would turn out at the end of the month.

I have helped companies who used the Flash Report format below to focus and prioritize financial reports for executive management and even the board of directors. They valued a snapshot that suggested what areas needed to be drilled into and to look for trends in key areas.

With my emphasis on cash and liquidity in this book, I included a Flash Report where key items to track are cash and working capital related. Tracking Accounts Receivable, Inventory, and Accounts Payable, combined with a ratio of interest coverage, suggests the strong emphasis on debt payment and watching balance sheet areas where cash could be consumed.

Three of the more common metrics for companies more concerned with the Income Statement than Balance Sheet issues are:

1. Sales backlog

2. New business booked

3. Number of employees

Depending upon your particular situation, you may separate my example below into a weekly summary of operating information and a financial statement summary type cover letter before financial statements.

Resources: The Doctor's Bag

NewCO
Monthly Flash Report
MONTH 200X

($000's)	YTD Ending 12/31/09	Budget YTD Ending 12/31/09	Prior YTD Ending 12/31/08	Month Ending x/31/2009	Budget Month Ending x/31/2009	Prior Month Ending x/31/2008
Sales						
% variance/ growth						
Gross Profit						
Gross Profit Margin						
EBITDA						
% margin						
% variance/ growth						
Interest Coverage						
Capital Expenditures						
Net Debt						
Net Debt/ EBITDA						
Accounts Receivable						
Inventory						
Accounts Payable						
Company Specific Drivers:						
Current Month Preview:						
Revenue						
EBITDA						
Especially Noteworthy Events:						

PLEASE REVIEW AND ADJUST FOR YOUR SITUATION BEFORE USING

R3 More Quantitative Approach to Risk Tolerance

Additional tips for Chapter 3

Wikipedia elaborates on risk tolerance with this combination of definition and examples, as a starting point for readers interested in more quantified approaches to risk tolerance.

A person is given the choice between two scenarios, one certain and one not. In the certain scenario, the person receives $50. In the uncertain scenario, a coin is flipped to decide whether the person receives $100 or nothing. The expected payoff for both scenarios is $50, meaning that an individual who was insensitive to risk would not care whether he or she took the certain payment or the gamble. However, individuals may have different risk attitudes. A person is:

- Risk averse if he or she would accept a payoff of less than $50 (for example, $40), with no uncertainty, rather than taking the gamble and possibly receiving nothing.

- Risk neutral if he or she is indifferent between the bet and a certain $50 payment.

- Risk seeking (or risk loving) if the guaranteed payment must be more than $50 (for example, $60) to induce him or her to take the certain option, rather than taking the gamble and possibly winning $100.

The average payoff of the gamble, known as its expected value, is $50. The dollar amount that the individual would accept instead of the bet is called the certainty equivalent, and the difference between the certainty equivalent and the expected value is called the risk premium.

Risk aversion is a concept in economics, finance, and psychology related to the behavior of consumers and investors under uncertainty. Risk aversion is the reluctance of a person to accept a bargain with an uncertain payoff rather than another bargain with a more certain, but possibly lower, expected payoff.

The inverse of a person's risk aversion is sometimes called risk tolerance.

R4 Levels of Accounting Resources

Additional tips for Chapter 5

Once the mission and vision are tweaked, CEOs and executives are faced with the issue of implementing their new plan or completing a key project. Often that requires extensive help from accounting or finance. That raises the question of what to expect from the levels of the accounting staff. For the purposes of this discussion, the following sections provide a basic definition of the players and a fuller description of what a CFO and Controller does. This definition provides a position description write-up for internal documentation or recruiting purposes.

Who Does What—Position Description

A *CFO* makes the financials understandable. This person ranges from a true business partner to a technician.

A *Controller* is a working manager for the accounting department. This person ranges from someone on the CFO track to a technician.

An *Accountant* gets the work done. This person is possibly certified or degreed.

An *Accounting Clerk/Bookkeeper* keeps the books. This person ranges from someone with minimal bookkeeping skills and clerical duties to office manager capabilities for early growth.

Job Descriptions

Being a CFO is a little like being a jack-of-all-trades. The following is a list of some (but not inclusive) of the main duties this position should cover. Of course because every company is different and there are always unique situations, more duties may be added to this list at any time or the priority of the listing changed for your particular needs.

CFO Duties:

- Is a key member of the executive team

- Manages accounting and finance functions

- Oversees strategic applications of budgeting and planning

- Interfaces with external professionals on insurance, compensation design, and taxes

- Acts as liaison with bankers and other financing sources

- Suggests optimal financing options

- Safeguards assets

- Can manage information technology in non-technology companies

- Upgrades product costing or bidding process

- Supervises the Controller or Accountant(s) and Bookkeeper(s)

- Sometimes manages administrative functions or purchasing

- Implements more professional financial and accounting systems

- Approves financial statements

- Coordinates with external CPA on tax returns, compilations, or audits

- Creates policies and procedures for implementation

- Oversees budgeting process

- Creates sophisticated cash management

- Can sign checks in addition to or instead of Controller or Owner

- Approves journal entries

A key question that may arise when working with a part-time CFO is, "When is it important to hire him or her on more than an outsourced basis?"

The general rule of thumb is that you know it's time to hire full-time help when the company grows enough that the amount being spent on the external CPA or part-time CFO suggests this work should be brought back in house. Often external equity financing sources will require this position be filled and may suggest specific candidates. Other deciding events may be one or more of the following: There's a need to speed up financial statements; more sophisticated cash flow monitoring, budgets or variance analysis is needed; your banker or CPA firm is telling you the position is needed; the owner wants to leverage his or her time with a key number two person.

Another good question to ask is, "What are the best resources to tap when we're searching for a CFO?"

The best way to fill all the accounting positions is by getting a referral from an existing CPA, law firm, or interim CFO, or your prior experience. A recruiter specializing in executive-level financial positions adds value in situations like specialized industries, substantial growth, or major financing needs.

Controllers also have highly specialized duties that require a variety of multitasking skills. Again because every company is different and there are always unique situations, more duties may be added to this list at any time or as the priorities of your company change.

Controller Duties:

- Prepares financial statements

- Implements basic financial and accounting systems

- Implements polices and procedures

- Begins safeguarding assets

- Creates budgets

- Can coordinate with external CPA on tax returns, compilations, or audits

- Creates non-standard reports, including variance reviews

- Handles insurance and risk management with assistance

- Approves customer credit limits

- Manages accountant(s) and bookkeeper(s)

- Handles executive payroll

- Can sign checks prepared by bookkeeper

- Signs sales tax returns

- Creates the more difficult journal entries
- Responsible for payroll processing

Again, there may come a time when the company needs to ask the question, "When should we hire on more than an outsourced basis?"

Basically, the same answer from the CFO question applies here as well. When the company grows enough that the amount being spent on the external bookkeeper, CPA, or part-time controller or part-time CFO suggests this work should be brought back in house. Other deciding events may be one or more of the following: financials are received more than 15 working days after month end, budgets are desired; variance analysis is needed; there is a need to speed up accounts receivable collections; or your banker or CPA firm is telling you the position is needed.

Where Should Our Company Find a Controller?

Again, the best way to fill all the accounting positions is by getting a referral from an existing CPA, a law firm, interim controller or CFO. In other cases like specialized industries, a recruiter specializing in mid-level accounting positions adds value.

 R5 Valuation

Additional tips for Chapter 6

Non-financial executives privately often ask for an overview or simple approach they can use to estimate corporate or project value if strategic objectives are met. I created the example below to influence growth clients to create at least $20 million of revenue since that is the point at which buyers give a higher value than lower revenue levels. Feel free to add zeros or change the ratios for your particular situation. Please check with your CPA to make it more meaningful for your exact situation.

Target
Valuation based on Year 5 projections of after tax net income at various multiples

Year 5 revenues	21,000,000
Year 5 EBITDA	3,780,000
Year 5 after tax net income	3,780,000

Multiple of PE	Projected Value	Multiple of EBITDA	Projected Value	Multiple of Revenues	Projected Value
3	9,450,000	4	15,120,000	0.75	15,750,000
4	12,600,000	5	18,900,000	1	21,000,000
5	15,750,000	6	22,680,000	1.5	31,500,000
6	18,900,000	7	26,460,000	2	42,000,000
7	22,050,000	8	30,240,000	2.5	52,500,000
8	25,200,000	9	34,020,000	3	63,000,000

Valuation does not include distribution of cash, accounts receivable etc less liabilities.
A strategic buyer may pay a higher multiple of Price Earnings because of unique value for them.

Obtain input values from your CPA or banker.

Distribution of Proceeds

Often those non-financial executives privately ask for a simple way to look at the proceeds they may receive after some form of external financing or partnership allocation is satisfied. The example below shows potential differences for financing where time or guaranteed multiples are involved and demonstrates how those forms of financing influences money available to the regular shareholders.

Input sectors				Yield recap table - simple annual compounding	
Investment		3,350,000			
Common stock override		20%			
Sales value at time period selected		20,000,000			

Table recaps showing first dollars to preferred investors at different return rates and time periods

guaranteed return %	Year 1	2	3	4	5
8%	3,618,000	3,907,440	4,220,035	4,557,638	4,922,249
10%	3,685,000	4,053,500	4,458,850	4,904,735	5,395,209

guaranteed multiple approach					
2	6,700,000	6,700,000	6,700,000	6,700,000	6,700,000
3	10,050,000	10,050,000	10,050,000	10,050,000	10,050,000

Investor gets first dollars as shown above and then share in prorata allocation to common on remaining value.

Proceeds estimate:	Net sales value of	20,000,000
	Less allocated proceeds of (input value from tables above)	
	say 10% at end of year 4	4,904,735
	Subtotal available to common	15,095,265
	Additional dollars available to preferred	3,019,053
	Total proceeds to preferred	7,923,788

Obtain input values from your CPA or banker.

Resources: The Doctor's Bag

 **R6 Timing Is Everything**

Additional tips for Chapter 8

Now that we've answered some of the key questions about creating a more efficient and timely board package, the question of when to distribute the package may arise. This is a very important decision due to the significantly higher effort needed to accelerate completion of that package for each additional day it is available to directors. After conducting an informal survey over the last two years, I've determined the time frame for what I believe is a reasonable and timely delivery of material. To this end, I have created three categories of companies including public, private and non-profit.

- Silver-level companies distribute their packages five working days before a board meeting.

- Gold-level companies earn this designation by distribute their packages six working days before a board meeting.

- Platinum-level companies send out board packages seven working days before a meeting. After seven days, executives have told me that the data begins to look dated.

You may have the same thoughts as some people have when I talk to them in person. "Those levels are too arbitrary and unrealistic." Chapter Eight describes the NACD survey which describes how much higher the bar is than my categories for public companies, and those private companies who adopt corporate governance similar to SEC reporting levels.

R7 Follow-On Tactical-Level Planning for Green Energy at Your Company
Additional tips for Chapter 10

After a basic "green energy" process and plan is in place, some companies will move to some follow-on version of fuller planning. The following is a template designed to examine seven clean energy considerations through self-evaluation. After taking it, you should have a better understanding of the impact primary foreseeable factors have on your company in terms of renewable energy. The quiz includes four pain points and a series of foreseeable changes that should be considered within the next three to five years. You fill in the blank for X with numbers your company should strategically consider.

1. *If the price of gasoline increased, what would happen within your business? It would:*

    ○ Be handled in stride until it reached what dollar amount?

    ○ Be inconvenient and impact the ability of executives and employees to maintain their bonus and incentive payments at what dollar amount?

    ○ Require us to find continuing savings elsewhere to cover this crucial area.

    ○ Substantially affect our corporate financial model without making major strategic changes at what dollar amount?

Resources: **145**
The Doctor's Bag

2. *If the average days delivery time element between order receipt to customer delivery increased, it would:*

   ○ Be handled in stride until the increase time approached how many extra days?

   ○ Be inconvenient and impact the ability of executives and employees to maintain their bonus and incentive payments, without a bottom line impact; for how many extra days?

   ○ Require us to find continuing savings elsewhere to cover this crucial area, at how many extra days?

   ○ Substantially affect our corporate financial model without making major strategic changes at how many extra days?

3. *If energy costs rose from a baseline 2008 level, it would:*

   ○ Be handled in stride at; 10%; 20%; 30%; 40%, or 50%

   ○ Be inconvenient and impact the ability of executives and employees to maintain their bonus and incentive payments, without a bottom line impact; at 10%; 20%; 30%; 40%, or 50%

   ○ Require us to find continuing savings elsewhere to cover this crucial area, at; 10%; 20%; 30%; 40%, or 50%

   ○ Substantially affect our corporate financial model without making major strategic changes at 10%; 20%; 30%; 40%, or 50%

4. **If regulators mandated a given percent decrease in carbon emission levels, it would:**

   ○ Be handled in stride at; 5%; 10%; 15%; 20%, or 25%

   ○ Be inconvenient and impact the ability of executives and employees to maintain their bonus and incentive payments, without a bottom line impact; at 5%; 10%; 15%; 20%, or 25%

   ○ Require us to find continuing savings elsewhere to cover this crucial area, at; 5%; 10%; 15%; 20%, or 25%

   ○ Substantially affect our corporate financial model without making major strategic changes at 5%; 10%; 15%; 20%, or 25%

5. **If regulators mandated a carbon tax credit system, it would:**

   ○ Be handled in stride at; at what level of additional regulation?

   ○ Be inconvenient and impact the ability of executives and employees to maintain their bonus and incentive payments, without a bottom line impact; at what level of additional regulation?

   ○ Require us to find continuing savings elsewhere to cover this crucial area, at what level of additional regulation?

   ○ Substantially affect our corporate financial model without making major strategic changes at what level of additional regulation?

6. *If the increase above our present blended interest rate on the coupon rate on new borrowings increased, it would:*

○ Being handled in stride at; ½%; 1%; 1.5%; 2%; or 2.5%

○ Be inconvenient and impact the ability of executives and employees to maintain their bonus and incentive payments, without a bottom line impact; at ½%; 1%; 1.5%; 2%; or 2.5%

○ Require us to find continuing savings elsewhere to cover this crucial area, at; ½%; 1%; 1.5%; 2%; or 2.5%

○ Substantially affect our corporate financial model without making major strategic changes at ½%; 1%; 1.5%; 2%; or 2.5%

7. *If our present policy toward renewable energy was reviewed by our local or regional paper commenting on how we compare to a "Ben & Jerry" type plan, it would:*

○ Being handled in stride; yes or no.

○ Be inconvenient and impact the ability of executives and employees to maintain their bonus and incentive payments, without a bottom line impact; yes or no.

○ Require us to find continuing savings elsewhere to cover this crucial area; yes or no.

○ Substantially affect our corporate financial model without making major strategic changes; yes or no.

For those who want to supplement this with a limited number of key strategic questions for self-analysis, consider these issues:

1. How will your corporate board prepare for a changing business environment vis-à-vis green energy legislation and initiatives?

2. How can a supply chain company "re-engineer" its business model to compete in a clean energy world?

3. What are the main challenges the clean energy sector must overcome to make it viable?

4. What are the global market implications of a green energy world in light of China's energy consumption and consumers' concerns about escalating energy costs?

5. What regulatory measures or legislation in the next congressional session will best serve American industries?

 R8 Carbon Tax at the Source

Additional tips for Chapter 10

Given the speed at which the green movement is taking hold as a critical business concern in the United States, I've been asked for my opinion on how American companies will be impacted by the green economy. Global trade is one area where the green economy will put American companies at a competitive disadvantage if the carbon tax does not counteract the lax emission standards of foreign countries with whom the United States does trade.

In this regard, I propose levying a carbon tax on products sold to Americans "at the source." In other words, products from another country that has lower emission standards than our country would pay an equivalent amount of green tax as part of the sale of the product in the United States.

Half of the tax collected on the foreign component of this carbon tax would go into a Social Security "lockbox." The other half would be dedicated to incentivizing a green energy transition and offsetting business transition costs of going green.

R9 Definitions

- *Balanced Scorecard* balances strategic non-financial performance measures to traditional financial metrics
- *C-Level* is normally used for the suite of Chief Officers (e.g., CEO, CFO, COO)
- *Carbon taxes* (which is really what a cap-and-trade system is)
- Customer relationship management (*CRM*)
- Enterprise Risk Management (*ERM*)
- Enterprise resource planning (*ERP*)
- Financial planning and analysis process (*FP&A*) function
- *Flash Report* is used most often when the report is prepared quickly before full financial data is available
- *Infrastructure* includes people skills, systems and facilities
- *Metrics* are critical success factors
- National Association of Corporate Directors (*NACD*)
- National Renewable Energy Laboratory website (*www.nrel.gov*)

R10 Personal Notes

R10 Personal Notes

R10 Personal Notes

R11 First Action to Take

Either while reading chapter 11 or elsewhere in the book, what three items did you note that would improve your business or reduce risk? Pick the most important of the three top actions to take and answer the following items to create an action plan.

What is the first action you plan to take?

_____

_____

_____

Why is this action important?

_____

_____

_____

What is the first step you need to take?

_____

_____

_____

When will this first step occur?

_____

Who can you get to help with the action?

_____

When does the action need to be completed?

_____

_____

How will you know the process was completed as planned?

_____

_____

_____

What potential benefits are you targeting in dollars and other benefits?

_____

_____

_____

R11 Second Action to Take

Moving forward, pick the second of your three top actions to take and answer the same following items to create another action plan.

What is the first action you plan to take?

_____
_____
_____

Why is this action important?

_____
_____
_____

What is the first step you need to take?

_____
_____
_____

When will this first step occur?

_____

Who can you get to help with the action?

_____

When does the action need to be completed?

_____

_____

How will you know the process was completed as planned?

_____

_____

_____

What potential benefits are you targeting in dollars and other benefits?

_____

_____

_____

R11 Third Action to Take

Finally, pick the third of your three top actions to take and answer the following items to create your final action plan.

What is the first action you plan to take?

_____
_____
_____

Why is this action important?

_____
_____
_____

What is the first step you need to take?

_____
_____
_____

When will this first step occur?

_____

Who can you get to help with the action?

_____

When does the action need to be completed?

_____

_____

How will you know the process was completed as planned?

_____

_____

_____

What potential benefits are you targeting in dollars and other benefits?

_____

_____

_____

R12 Do You Have a Question?

To talk with Gary Patterson about your business: This book covers a range of issues for high-growth companies and enterprise risk management concerns. A number of these issues can be discussed or researched in much more detail. If you have an issue you would like to discuss or suggestions for another book or service, please go to

www.fiscaldoctor.com/contact.html

and let Gary know how you prefer to be contacted. While you're at the contact page, request a free copy of the FiscalDoctor's Due Diligence Checklist, which is useful for operational assessments and enterprise risk management.

For updates on enterprise risk management: Gary Patterson blogs about ERM and other timely business concerns at:

www.fiscalclinic.com

To apply these Best Practices to your business: Gary Patterson can:

- Work with companies, worldwide on short-term or retainer-based projects
- Discuss your business problems, questions or comments
- Facilitate strategy or planning sessions
- Develop one-on-one coaching or mentoring
- Give a tailored speech on issues relevant to your situation
- Introduce his affiliates to your company
- Estimate the cost of what you don't know